OUTLINE-HISTORY OF GREEK RELIGION

OUTLINE-HISTORY OF GREEK RELIGION

BY

LEWIS RICHARD FARNELL, M.A., D.Litt.

RECTOR OF EXETER COLLEGE, OXFORD; GIFFORD LECTURER AT THE UNIVERSITY OF
ST. ANDREWS; FORMERLY WILDE LECTURER IN NATURAL AND COMPARATIVE
RELIGION IN THE UNIVERSITY OF OXFORD; HIBBERT LECTURER; HON. D.
LITT. OF THE UNIVERSITY OF GENEVA, TRINITY COLLEGE, DUBLIN, AND
UNIVERSITY OF ST. ANDREWS; AUTHOR OF "CULTS OF THE GREEK
STATES," "THE EVOLUTION OF RELIGION," "HIGHER ASPECTS
OF GREEK RELIGION," "GREECE AND BABYLON"

ARES   PUBLISHERS   INC.
CHICAGO   MCMLXXIV

Unchanged Reprint of the Edition:
London, 1921.
ARES   PUBLISHERS   INC.
150 E. Huron Street
Chicago, Illinois 60611
Printed in the United States of America
International Standard Book Number:
0-89005-025-2
Library of Congress Catalog Card Number:
74-77882

CONTENTS

OUTLINE-HISTORY OF GREEK RELIGION

CHAPTER I

THE SOURCES AND THE EVIDENCE

THE foundation of a serious and scientific study of Greek religion, as distinct from the mere mythology of Hellas, may almost be said to have been an achievement of the last generation of scholars. And it is only through recent research that the Hellenic spirit, so creative and imperial in the domains of literature, art and science, can be recognised as manifesting itself not unworthily in the sphere of religion.

The history of Greek religion means, partly, the account and the interpretation of the various rites, cults and cult-ideas of the various Greek families, tribes and communities ; partly the estimate of the religious temperament, both of the masses and of the individuals who emerged from among them and of whom some record has been preserved.

Now as the Greek world in the long period of its independence was never organised as a single State, the attempt to give a summary and general account of its religion is confronted with the perplexity arising from the often incalculable diversity of religious forms and ideas in the different centres of its social life, which was in the highest degree centrifugal. Nevertheless, as will be shown, we find in the midst of manifold local variation certain uniformity of religious psychology, making for uniformity of practice, which enables us to deliver certain general pronouncements about the whole.

Ancient Sources : Literary.—Our real knowledge of any ancient religion depends obviously on the copiousness and variety of our records. And it is likely to be more luminous, if the society in question expressed its religious life not only in surviving literature, but also in surviving art. Of both these kinds the student of Greek religion has an unusually rich material.

For in spite of its secular freedom, which is its salient achievement, Greek literature in its highest and most popular forms, as well as in its narrower and more special, is deeply infused or preoccupied with religion and religious myth. In fact, it reflects the vivifying penetration of religion into all parts of Greek activity and mental life. This is obviously true of the epic period, which produced the two types of the chivalrous and the theologic epic, and which has left us most valuable material for the religious history of the tenth and ninth centuries in the Homeric poems, and of the eighth and seventh centuries in the poems of Hesiod and in the 'Homeric' hymns. It is none the less true of the great lyric movement that followed upon that, when the greatest poets devoted themselves to the composition of songs for festal-religious occasions or of hymns for the service of temple or altar ; and besides these whose great names and fragments of whose great works survive, there was another less distinguished group of special ' hieratic ' poets, such as Pamphos and Mousaios, who composed hymns for the service of certain mystery-cults, and whose compositions were preserved as liturgical documents by the priestly families that administered them.

The sententious ethical-political poetry of the sixth century, the elegiacs of Theognis and Solon, is instinct with religious emotion and reflection. And the greatest product of the poetic genius of Hellas, the tragic drama, is of a religious character, both in respect of its origin and much of its subject-matter. Finally, the later learned poetry of the Ptolemaic period, the Kassandra of Lycophron, the hymns and other works of Kallimachos, the epic poem of Apollonios Rhodios, are full of antiquarian religious lore.

At the same time, our knowledge is much indebted to the great prose-writers of Greece, the philosophers, historians and orators ; among the philosophers, especially to Plato, who more copiously than any of the others reveals to us, however much he idealises, the religious psychology and cult-phenomena of his period ; among the historians, especially to Herodotus, who is the intellectual ancestor of the modern anthropologist and student of comparative religion and whose presentation of the facts is coloured with religious conviction. The works of the Attic orators are of special value for our purpose, first because the classical orator was far more apt than the modern to dilate on religious themes and appeal to religious sentiments, as religion was far more closely interfused with political and social life ; secondly, because we are more sure of the orator than we can be of the poetic or philosophic writer that his words are attuned to the average pitch of popular belief and sentiment.

It is true then that all the great fields of Greek literature make their several contributions to the material of our subject. And besides the works of the great masters, the student has to reckon with the secondary and parasitic work of the later scholiasts, compilers and commentators, which is even more replete with the special information upon which the history of Greek religion can be built. The study of it is, in fact, almost coextensive with the whole study of Greek literature.

But amidst this profusion of material we must specially mark the works of those ancients who wrote direct treatises on the various religious phenomena, on the Gods, the cult-practices, the theologic and mythologic systems of the Hellenic societies. The earliest of such works that have come down to us are the poems of Hesiod and the Hesiodic school, the Works and Days and the Theogony, while of parts of the ' Homeric ' hymns the special theme is the attributes and functions of the various divinities. But it was not till the period of scientific activity after Aristotle that definite treatises in prose on different departments of the national religion began to be rife. A chapter on sacrifice by Theophrastos is mainly preserved for us by Porphyry. The writers of ' Atthides ' or Attic history and antiquities, who belonged mainly to the third century, were special workers in this field ; Philochoros, the chief of them, wrote ' on festivals,' ' on sacred days,' ' on divination,' ' on the Attic mysteries ' ; Istros, the slave and friend of Kalli-machos, on the ' manifestations of Apollo ' and on

' the Cretan sacrifices ' ; while the ' exegetic work '
of Kleidemos was, if we may judge from the fragments that remain, occupied with the problems of
religion and mythology.   Outside this circle we hear
of other contributions to the history of Greek
religion, such as the treatises of Herakleides, probably the pupil of Aristotle, usually called ' Pontikos,'
on ' the foundations of temples,' and ' on oracles ' ;
and a work by an unknown Sokrates of Kos on the
important subject of ' Invocation-titles of the Gods.'
Lastly may be mentioned here a treatise of Apollodoros, ' περι Θεων,' which, if he is to be identified
with the author of the ' Bibliotheca,' was probably
a learned account of the popular religion rather than
a metaphysical enquiry.

Of nearly all this scientific post-Aristotelian
literature only isolated fragments survive in quota-
tions by later writers, lexicographers, and scholiasts,
who were no doubt more deeply indebted to it than
they always acknowledged ; but it is some com-
pensation for our loss that the work last mentioned,
the Bibliotheca of Apollodoros, has been preserved,
a rich storehouse of myth and folklore with some
infusion of actual cult-record.   Among the later
literature our subject is indebted to the geographer,
Strabo, for many incidental observations of local
cults and ritual ; still more to the philosophic
moralist and littérateur, Plutarch, a man of earnest
religious interest and some power of. original
thought, who knew the religion of his country at
first hand and at a time when it was yet alive, and
who devoted to it much attention and literary
industry ; hence we must rank high among our
ancient authorities his Quæstiones Græcæ and his

treatises 'on the Pythian Oracle' and on 'the cessation of oracles.' Again, much desultory but varied information is afforded by the compilers Athenæus, in his *Deipnosophistæ*, and Stobæus, in his *Florilegium*. But of higher value than all these, or in fact than any work that has been bequeathed to us from antiquity, is the *Descriptio Græciæ*, by Pausanias, composed about 180 A.D. ; for he travelled somewhat as a modern anthropologist, relying partly on earlier literature, yet using his own eyes and ears and his own notes ; and his ruling passion was the study of the folk-religion and the religious monuments ; so that it is due mainly to him that we know something of the village-religion of Hellas as distinct from that of the great cities, and can frame working theories of the evolution through immemorial ages of various growths of the polytheism.

The lexicographers Harpokration, Hesychios and Suidas contribute facts of value, especially in their citation of cult-appellatives, which owing to the magic value of the special name or title whereby the deity was invoked throw a revealing light on the significance and power of many a worship, and help to frame our conception of the complex character of many a divinity. Again, the various collections of ' Scholia ' on the classical texts are a rich quarry for our reconstruction of the fabric of Hellenic religion ; and of chief value among these are the Scholia on Homer, Pindar, Æschylus, Euripides, Aristophanes and Theocritus, while Servius' *Commentary on Vergil* tells us even more about Greek cult and mythology than about Roman ; and high in this class of our authorities we must rank a work of late Byzantine learning, the *Commentary of Tzetzes* on Lykophron's poem, ' Kassandra,' for his scholia are charged with remote antiquarian lore derived from good sources.

Finally, we gather much of our knowledge from the controversial treatises of the early Christian Fathers, written with propagandist zeal in the heat of their struggle against Paganism. They reveal to us much of the religion that they strove to overthrow by the exposure of its viciousness and its absurdities. But their statements must be used with cautious criticism. Their knowledge was by no means always at first hand, unless—which we rarely know to have been the case—they were, like Clemens of Alexandria, converted Pagans who had been bred up in the Græco-Roman polytheism. Their statements, for instance, about the Greek mysteries are often vague and unconvincing, while in their desire to include them all in one general condemnation they confuse Anatolian rites with Eleusinian. And they are pardonably blind to the often beautiful ritual, the nobler ideas and the higher moral elements in the older Mediterranean religions. Nevertheless, if we make due allowance for prejudice and exaggeration, works such as the *Protreptica* of Clemens, the treatise of Arnobius, *Adversus Gentes*, of Firmicus Maternus, *De Errore Profanarum Gentium*, Eusebius' *Præparatio Evangelica*, Augustine's *De Civitate Dei*, Athenagoras' *Legatio*, must be ranked among the primary sources of our history.

A special but very important chapter in the later history of Greek religion is the account of the growth and diffusion of the religious brotherhoods, especially the Orphic Dionysiac societies. For these we have something of direct liturgical evidence in the collection of Orphic hymns, mainly the products of the later theosophic period, but throwing light on the theology and ritual of these sects. But our knowledge of this mystic religion which was engrafted upon Hellenism has been in recent times enriched by the priceless discovery of an ancient poetical Orphic liturgy engraved upon gold-leaf found in tombs of Crete and South Italy and probably a product of the fifth century B.C.

Monumental.—The above is a sketch of our more important literary sources. The knowledge to be derived from them would, on the whole and in many important details, remain vague and uncertain, were it not supplemented and secured by the evidence coming from another source which we may term semi-literary, the evidence from inscriptions. These have been accumulated in vast profusion during the last thirty years, and have been, and are still being, reduced to order for our special purpose. The public inscriptions, being dry state-documents, do not reveal to us the heart of any mystery or the religious soul of the people, but rather the State-organisation and the exact minutiæ of ritual and sacrifice from which we can sometimes reconstruct an image of the inward religious thought. And many a local cult of value for our total impression that was unrecorded by any writer is revealed to us by these monuments. But the needs and aspirations of the private man are better attested by the private inscriptions attached to ex-voto dedications or commemorating divine benefits received.

Yet amidst all this wealth of evidence there seems one thing lacking. Of actual temple-liturgies, of formal prayers proffered round the altars, of the hymns chanted in the public service, of all that might constitute a text of Greek church-service there is comparatively little preserved. One or two hymns and a few fragments of the religious lyric of the seventh century—to which we may now add the important recent find of the pæans of Pindar—a strophe of an ancient hymn to Dionysos sung by the Elean women, a fourth-century pæan to Dionysos composed for the Delphic service, the newly discovered hymn of the Kouretes in Crete, a few formulæ of prayers quoted or paraphrased by later writers—all this appears meagre material when we compare it with the profusion of documents of the public and private religion that are streaming in from Babylon.

But in respect of another source of the history of religion, our Greek material is unique, namely, the monuments of art. For the greatest art of Hellas was mainly religious, the greatest artists working for the religious service of the State. And the surviving works of sculpture, painting and glyptic, wrought either for public or private purposes, present us often not only with facts of religion and ritual unrecorded in literature, but also with an impression hard to gain otherwise of the religious consciousness of the people and serve also as witnesses to the strength of the religious feeling. For instance, the knowledge and appreciation of Athena's personality that we derive from Attic monuments is deeper and more vivid than any that we gain from the literature. Therefore the study of Greek religion is concerned as much with the art and archæology as with the literature.

CHAPTER II

THE PREHISTORIC PERIOD

A SUMMARY sketch of so manifold a theme as that with which this short handbook deals will be of more value if it can present the facts in some kind of chronologic sequence.

We may conveniently distinguish four periods : the first, the prehistoric, falling mainly in the second millennium B.C. and closing with the epoch marked by the Homeric poems ; the second, extending from 900 to 500 B.C., beginning with the colonial expansion of Hellas and ending before the Persian invasion; the third, from 500 to 338 B.C., including the greatest century of Greek history and closing with the battle of Chæronea and the establishment of Macedonian supremacy ; the fourth and last, the Hellenistic and Græco-Roman period.

The chronologic statement is embarrassed by the absence of any record of date for the institution and diffusion of most of the cults and for the growth of certain religious ideas ; nor can we safely date a religious fact by the date of the author who first mentions it ; a detail of ritual, a myth, a religious concept, only attested by Pausanias or a late scholiast, may descend from an age centuries before the Homeric. And our earliest inscriptions do not as yet reach back to a period earlier than the beginning of the seventh century.

For determining our view of Greek religion in the second millennium B.C., when Hellenism was in the making, the poems of Homer and Hesiod are of priceless value if they are used with cautious and trained criticism. We depend greatly also on the general inductions of comparative religion and anthropology, which may sometimes guide us rightly in this matter, especially if the anthropological comparison is drawn from more or less adjacent communities rather than from the Antipodes. We depend also on the evidence of the monuments of the Minoan-Mycenæan religion, revealing glimpses of the practices and faith of a people of high culture, whom no one would dare now to call, at least in the earlier stage of their life, Hellenic, but from whom the earliest Hellenes doubtless adopted much into their own religion.

Sketch of Homeric religion.—The poems of Homer present us with an advanced polytheism, a system in which the divinities are already correlated in some sort of hierarchy and organised as a divine family under a supreme God. These divine beings are not mere ' daimones ' or ' numina,' such as were in the main the old deities of Rome, vague and dimly outlined forces animate yet scarcely personal ; but rather concrete and individual Θεοί of robust and sharply defined personality, not spirits but immortal beings of superhuman substance and soul, conceived in the glorified image of man. The anthropomorphic bias is dominant in the poems, plastically shaping the figures of all the divinities, except occasionally some of the lower grade, such as

B

the river-god Skamandros. Even the vague group
of nymphs, female ' daimones ' of the rill and the
mountain, while lacking individual characterisation,
bear the anthropomorphic name, ' Brides,' or
' young women,' which is the root-meaning of
Νύμφη. Though the gods and goddesses are shape-
shifters and may manifest or disguise themselves in
the form of any animal—birds by choice—yet their
abiding type is human; nor has Homer any clear
remembrance of a ' cow-faced ' Hera, still less of an
' owl-faced ' Athena, since for him at least ' Hera
βοῶπις ' was Hera ' of the large ox-eyes '—the term
is a complimentary epithet of women—and Athena
γλαυκῶπις, the goddess ' of the flashing eyes.' Also
his divinities are moralised beings with human
passions and ethical as well as artistic emotions.
The highest among them are not imagined as
Nature-powers, bound up with or immanent in the
forces and departments of the natural world, for
such a description applies only to his wind-Gods and
nymphs and gods of river and sea ; also, though
more loosely, to his Helios, the God of the Sun ; to
beings in fact that count little in his religious world.
It scarcely applies to Poseidon, for though his
province is the sea, and some of his functions and
appellatives ' the girdler of the earth,' ' the earth-
shaker,' ' he of the dark blue locks ' are derived from
it, he is also the builder of the walls of Troy, the
family deity of the house of Nestor, and the God of
horses. It does not describe at all his mode of
imagining and presenting Apollo, Hera, Athena,
Hermes and others. There is no hint that these
divinities were conceived by him as nature-powers
or as evolved from any part of the natural world.

The High God, Zeus, though specially responsible
for the atmospheric and celestial phenomena, is not
identified with the thunder or even with the sky,
though a few phrases may reveal the influence of
an earlier animistic conception of the divine sky.
His religious world, in short, is morphologically
neither a system of polydaimonism nor one of
pantheism in which a divine force is regarded as
universally immanent in the world of things ; but is
constructed on the lines of personal theism.

We may observe also that the polytheism of the
age of Perikles in regard to some of its leading
divinities has not markedly advanced beyond the
Homeric. Athena, in the Homeric poems, is already
the Goddess of war, arts, and counsel ; and there
are already hints in the Homeric presentation of her
of the tender Madonna-like character that is beautifully developed in the later Attic monuments. The
Homeric Apollo is already the oracular God who
delights in the music of the Pæan, though his
artistic and intellectual character is not yet fully
developed. Of Hermes and Hephaistos the later
Attic conception is not notably different from the
Homeric.

Again, in spite of one or two frivolous and
licentious passages, the religious tone in the Homeric
poems is serious and in many important respects
accords with an advanced morality. The deity,
though jealous and revengeful of wrongs or slights
to himself, is on the whole on the side of righteous-
ness and mercy ; his displeasure is aroused by those
who spurn the voice of prayer, who injure the
suppliant, the guest, or even the beggar ; and
besides Zeus and the other ' Olympians,' who are

general guardians of the right, there loom the dark
powers of the lower world, who are specially concerned with the sanctity of the oath. Much also of
the religious reflection in the poems strikes us as
mature and advanced : notably that passage at the
beginning of the Odyssey where Zeus declares that
it is not the Gods who bring evil to men, but that it
is the wickedness of their own hearts that is the
cause of all their evils.

Finally, the Homeric ritual appears as on the
higher level of theism. We can detect it in no trace
of savagery and but little contamination of the
religion with magic. The sacrifice is more than a
mere bribe ; it is a friendly communion with the
divinity ; and the service is solemn and beautiful
with hymn and dance. The cult is furnished with
altar and sometimes with temple and a priesthood,
but not yet, as a rule, with the idol, though this is
beginning to appear.

This slight sketch of Homeric theology is presented
here in the belief that the Homeric poems enable us
to catch some glimmer of the religion of the centuries
preceding the first millennium. This belief is based
on the conviction that the poems represent a Greek
society existing near the date of 1000 B.C. It is of
course opposed to the view still maintained by some
scholars that they are, in their finished form, a
product of a much later period, and that the religion
which they enshrine may be such as was in vogue in
Attica about the epoch of Peisistratos. But certain
arguments drawn from ethnology and sociology are
fatal to this theory, and still more so are the arguments that may be drawn from the history of Greek
religion ; for at the period of Peisistratos certain

religious forces were rife, and certain religious phenomena prominent, of which Homer is entirely silent.

Still less reasonable is it to imagine that Homer constructs a religious world out of his own brain. We must suppose that he reflects something real and contemporary. Only we must guard ourselves from the serious error of supposing that he reflects the whole. Much is doubtless missing in his account which we may be able to supply from Hesiod and other sources by means of reasonable hypotheses.

The assumption is, then, that the Homeric poems present us with a part-picture of the religion that prevailed among some of the leading Greek communities before the Dorian invasion of the Peloponnese and the Ionic colonisation of Asia Minor.

Pre-Homeric period of religion.—Now when we consider how slow of growth and enduring are the forms and the moral and metaphysical concepts of religion we have the right to believe that part of what Homer records on these matters is the inherited tradition of an age some centuries earlier than his own. It is probable that those earliest Aryan immigrants from the north, Achæans, Dryopes, Minyai and others—who by mingling with peoples of aboriginal Mediterranean stock and of the Minoan-Mycenæan culture constituted the happy blend that we call the Hellenic race—had already arrived at the stage of personal theism ; and that Hellenic religion proper does not start with a ' godless period '[1] when the unseen powers were only dimly outlined in the vaguer and more fleeting characters of what is

[1] As Karsten assumes in his *Outlines of Greek Religion*, p. 6.

called animism. We now know from the valuable discovery of a cuneiform inscription that the Iranian people had evolved such personal deities as Mitra and Varuna before 1400 B.C.[1] And we have the right to suppose that their western kinsfolk, who were forcing their way through the Balkans, probably only a century earlier, were at least at the same level of religious imagination. We can best understand the picture of the religious world of Homer and also the later cult-records, if we believe that the kindred tribes coming from the north brought in certain personal deities, some of whom were common to more than one stock, and one at least may have been common to them all. This would best explain the supremacy of Zeus, the Sky-God, the diffusion of his name Olympios, derived from the mountain that dominates the northern frontier, near to which the people that were to lead the history of Greece had at one time temporary settlements and which they regarded as the throne of their high God. The wide geographical area of his cult cannot be naturally explained on the assumption that at any period in Hellenic history he had been merely the special deity of one particular tribe. Also as regards two other high Gods at least, Apollo and Poseidon, we may be reasonably sure that already in the pre-Homeric period certain tribes other than the Achæans had these cult-figures. In the Hyperborean ritual, which reflects at points the earliest days of Hellenism, we can follow the track of Apollo's invasion from the north ; and the evidence is fairly clear that

---

[1] Vide E. Meyer, " Der erste auftreten der Aryer in der Geschichte," *Sitzungsb. d. König. preuss. Akad. Wissensch.*, 1908, p. 14.

Poseidon was equally a northern immigrant, being the special tribal deity of the Minyai.

We must not then apply to the pre-Homeric period of Greek religion the formula, ' one tribe one God,' but must imagine that religion had already surmounted in some degree the tribal barriers ; for though the spirit of tribal exclusiveness was strong throughout the earlier periods of this polytheism, certain families and certain tribes having the special prerogative of certain ἱερά and jealously excluding strangers, yet the fact of the common possession of certain worships by various tribes contained the germ of religious expansiveness.

Moreover, at some age indefinitely earlier than the Homeric, the conception of the high God had expanded both cosmically and ethically. Zeus had become more than a ' departmental God ' ; the deity of the sky was also in the first period—so far as we can reconstruct it—Zeus ' Chthonios,' the Lord of the life of earth and of the world under the earth, and it is likely that Hades was only an emanation from him. Also, we may regard the Homeric appellation of Zeus, πατὴρ ἀνδρῶν τε Θεῶν τε, as a conventional and crystallised phrase descending from an older poetic tradition. And we are justified in interpreting it as a phrase belonging to the higher plane of theism.[1]

We must also suppose that the anthropomorphic view of the personal deity, of which Homer is so attractive a spokesman, had asserted itself in the period before his. Unlike the early Roman, the early Hellenic divinities could be regarded as married, and ideas derived from the life of the

[1] Vide my *Hibbert Lectures*, p. 93.

family could be applied to them ; although we can
often discern that many of the myths concerning
divine relationships—the sisterhood of Artemis to
Apollo, for instance—do not belong to the earliest
Hellenic epoch.

Minoan-Mycenæan religion.—But any account of
the Hellenic polytheism of the second millennium
demands a critical study of the Minoan-Mycenæan
religion as well, and before we can decide what part
of the Homeric and later systems belongs to the
aboriginal Aryan-Hellenic tradition, we must know
what the northerners found indigenous in the lands
that they conquered or occupied. We know now
that they found in many centres a culture superior
to their own and a religion of an advanced theistic
type with elaborate, though mainly aniconic, ritual,
devoted pre-eminently to a Great Goddess, by whose
side a God was only the subordinate partner. It
has been pointed out[1] that where we find in historic
Greece the Goddess-cult predominant, and especially the prevalence of a virgin-goddess, we should
recognise the Minoan-Mycenæan tradition in
antagonism to the ' Aryan,' the latter invariably
maintaining the predominance of the God. We may
therefore believe the cults of Artemis in Arcadia and
Attica, of Athena in Attica, the cult—though not
the name—of Hera in Argos[2] and Samos, to have
been inherited from the former rather than to have
been brought in by the latter. And sometimes
linguistic science will be able to assign the different
personalities of the polytheism to its different

---

[1] Vide my *Greece and Babylon*, pp. 95–99.
[2] The name Hera is probably Aryan-Hellenic, but applied in
Argolis to the pre-Hellenic Goddess.

ethnic strains, by determining the group of languages to which the divine name in question belongs. Those that can be explained with certainty or probability as of ' Aryan ' or Indo-Germanic and may therefore be presumed to have penetrated Greece from the north, are Zeus, Hera, Ares, Demeter, Hestia, Dionysos, probably Poseidon and Apollo. On the other hand, ' Athena,' ' Artemis,' ' Aphrodite,' ' Hephaistos ' defy explanation on these lines, and probably belong to a primitive Ægean language. We may be doubtful about ' Hermes,' though elsewhere I have argued for his ' non-Hellenic ' origin. That philology has not yet brought us nearer to the solution of many of these problems is due to the lacunæ in our knowledge of the pre-Hellenic Mediterranean languages, and especially to our ignorance of the Minoan script for which we have masses of material but as yet no interpreter. Finally, the evidence of the early geographical area of a certain cult may sometimes be decisive in itself ; this is the case in regard to the cults of the ' Mother of the Gods ' and of Aphrodite, who are aboriginally connected with Crete and Cyprus respectively, that is, with the centres of the Minoan culture.

We assume then that the polytheism of the Greece of history was a blend of Northern and Mediterranean elements ; and the poems of Homer may reveal a reflection of the early Achæan period when the fusion was not yet fully accomplished. Thus we find there that Athena, Hephaistos, Hermes and the Goddess of Argos had been already ' Achæanised or Hellenised,' and are warm champions of the Hellenic cause ; while Artemis, Aphrodite, Ares, though genealogically linked to the Olympian family, are

equally warm on the side of Troy and are treated by
the poet with irreverence and even contumely. The
position of Apollo is different. There are over-
powering reasons for regarding him as of northern
origin, a genuinely Achæan deity, and the Achæan
poet treats him with deep respect. And we can only
explain his pro-Trojan sympathies by the assumption that when the poems were composed his cult
had become dominant on the Trojan shore, which
he was therefore supposed to guard.

But the ethnic decision is at present impossible on
a vast number of details in this composite polytheism, in respect both of ritual and of the divine
personalities ; and the student of Hellenic religion
must often abandon temporarily the quest of origins
in his investigation of the composite whole.

Proto-Hellenic period.—The very high development of this Mediterranean civilisation from which
Hellenism drew so much of its own life is in itself
sufficient reason for the belief that the advanced
picture that Homer presents of his contemporary
polytheism affords us a true estimate of the progress
that had been achieved in the centuries before him.
And this is corroborated by a careful analysis of the
later cult-records.

Family religion.—Society in the latter half of the
second millennium had already reached the higher
agricultural stage and had evolved the monogamic
family. Demeter—whose Aryan descent is proved
by her name—was generally recognised by the
various Hellenic tribes as the Earth-Goddess of corn,
and the very ancient festival of the Thesmophoria
was commonly associated with her. Certain forms
of the religion of the family, which was the life-

source of much of the private ethics of later Greece, can be traced back to the earliest period ; the worship, for instance, of Zeus Ἑρκεῖος, the God of the garth, around whose altar in the courtyard of the old Aryan house the kinsmen gathered for worship. Another sacred centre of the family life in the pre-Homeric Society was doubtless the hearth and the hearth-stone in the middle of the hall ; there are allusions to its sanctity in the Homeric poems, and the cult-records attest the great antiquity of this religious fact ; although the development of the personal goddess Hestia is a later phenomenon.

Again, the wider kinship-groups of the φρατρίαι and γένη are obviously pre-Homeric, and doubtless these had been consecrated by aboriginal religion, though we cannot date precisely the emergence of such cult-forms as Zeus Φράτριος and Athena Φρατρία, the deities who were specially concerned with the constitution and rights of the kindred-group.

Political religion.—Further, it is fairly clear that already in this first stage the religion had become closely interfused with the higher political and social life. Although the greater part of the population lived still under the tribal system in scattered villages—κωμηδόν—yet the ' polis ' had already arisen ; and in certain cases we may surmise for it a religious origin, where its name is derived from the personal name or the shrine of some divinity. Examples are ' Athenai,' Alalkomenai, Potniai, perhaps Megara. In these cases the temple must have been the nucleus around which grew up the secular habitations ; and the deity of the temple would become supreme in the political religion.

Athena had won this position at Athens and probably elsewhere in the immemorial pre-Homeric past ;
and this explains her character in the Homeric poem
as the divinity who more than all others inspires
political wisdom and counsel. Various indications
point in fact to the belief that the earliest development of the city life was closely bound up with the
cults of Zeus and Athena ; for no other divinity was
ever styled Polieus or Polias by any Greek State ;
and this agrees mainly with the presentation of
them in the Homeric poems. The unanimity of the
tradition points back to the second millennium, as
the period when this political characterisation of the
two deities was determined. And this view is
strikingly confirmed by the records concerning the
ritual and the establishment of the cult of Zeus
' Polieus ' on the Athenian Akropolis, an institution
attributed to Kekrops and marking probably the
Hellenisation of Attica ; the singular features of the
ritual and the association preserved in its legend of
Attica with Crete indicate a high antiquity, when
agriculture was the economic basis of the political as
well as the religious life.

We may believe that other cults besides the two
just mentioned played their part in the political
growth of the pre-Homeric world. The market-
place, the cradle of political oratory, had become
sacred ground, as Homer himself attests ; and this
consecration was probably marked by the presence
of some ' agalma,' a sacred stone of Hermes, for
instance. Apollo, also, had early divested himself
of the aboriginal character of the god of the wood
and of the homeless migratory host, had become a
builder of cities, and had established himself in the

city's streets with a change in the meaning of his
title, Αγυιεύς, once an appellative of the Way-God
who guided the host through the wild, now of the
deity who guarded the ways of the city. And
already, before Homer, his shrine at Pytho was
beginning to acquire wealth and political importance as an oracular centre of consultation.

Ethical religion.—The theistic system had been
turned to good account in other directions than the
political before it appeared on the canvas of Homer.
The whole morality of early social life had been
nurtured and protected by it ; for we may maintain
that the ethical religious spirit of Homer—unless we
regard him as a man or as a group of men to whom a
special revelation had been made—must reflect in
some degree a tradition that had grown up in the
centuries before him. We see then that current
conceptions about the Gods had ceased to be
inspired merely by fear ; a milder sentiment had
come to tinge religious thought ; the Deity was
regarded not only as a righteous God of vengeance,
but as loving mercy and compassion and as a
defender of the weak and destitute. Only once, and
only in regard to the wild sea-god Poseidon, does a
Homeric phrase suggest that the deity might have
been regarded as in his own nature malevolent.[1]
The cult of Zeus Ξείνιος, the guardian of the stranger
and the wanderer, had already arisen. And the
sanctity of the oath taken in the name of the deities
of the upper and the lower world was the basis of
much private and communal morality.

Art an aspect of religion.—And other parts of the
higher activity of man had been consecrated by the

[1] *Od.*, 13, 174.

polytheism of which Homer inherits and develops the tradition. The earliest imagination of the Hellenes appears to have perceived a daimoniac potency—a ' numen ' as we may say—in the arts of song and music ; and this had sometimes crystallised into the personal forms of divinities, into such interesting embodiments as the Muses or the Charites, who must have belonged to the pre-Homeric popular theism. The latter group had grown up at the Bœotian Orchomenos, an old centre of the Minoan-Mycenæan culture. It may be that at one time they had no other than the purely physical significance of vegetation-powers ; but we only understand their value for Homer if we suppose that before his time they had come to be associated with the arts and the delight of human life. We discern also that the higher deities, Apollo and Athena, though by no means merely ' functional ' or departmental powers, had acquired the special patronage of song and art. It seems, then, that in the earliest as in the later periods of their history the religion of the Hellenes idealised that sphere of human activity in which the Hellenic spirit was to achieve its highest, the sphere of art, and among higher and lower religions it was unique in this.

Proto-Hellenic ritual.—It seems, then, that even in the earliest period the polytheism was no longer on the most primitive plane. And we gather the same impression from what is revealed to us of the earliest forms of Greek ritual. The Homeric and Hesiodic poems are full of information concerning the liturgy or cult-service with which the poets were familiar ; what they tell us avails first of all for the period of the eleventh to the eighth century. But ritual takes long to develop, and once fixed is the most abiding element in religion. It is not too bold, then, to take the Homeric account as vouching for a tradition that goes back at least to the later centuries of the second millennium.

The sacred place of worship might be a natural cave, or a ' temenos,' a fenced clearing in a grove, containing as the ἄγαλμα of the deity a tree-trunk or holy pillar or heap of stones, whence gradually an artificial altar might be evolved ; the latter had become, some time before Homer, the usual receptacle of sacrifice and was a prominent figure in the Minoan-Mycenæan religion, which usually associated it with a sacred tree or pillar, the token of the deity's presence or a magnet for attracting it, but not with any iconic statue or idol. Personal religion could content itself with such equipment, but, if the anthropomorphic instinct is strong in it, it prompts the construction of the temple or the house of God. And temples must have been found in the land in the pre-Homeric period ; the few that have as yet been revealed in the area of Minoan-Mycenæan culture were built, with one exception,[1] within the royal palaces, and must be regarded as domestic chapels of the king, marking his sacred character as head of the religion of the State, the character with which the legends invest King Minos and King Aiakos. The earliest that have been excavated on free sites are the temples of Hera at Argos and Olympia, and these are now dated not earlier than the ninth century B.C. But the traditions of the earliest temple at Delphi, and of that of Athena on the

[1] At Gournia. Vide Hawes' *Crete the Forerunner of Greece,* pp. 101–102.

Athenian Acropolis, suggest a greater antiquity than this.

With the multiplication of temples special priest-hoods must also have multiplied. But the professional priest had already arisen in pre-Homeric times ; Homer knows of the brotherhood called the Selloi,[1] who tended the oracular oak of Zeus at Dodona, "who slept on the ground and never washed their feet," and he mentions others who were attached to special deities, and two of these at least administered cults without a temple, the priest of Zeus of Mount Ida,[2] and the priest of the river Skamandros,[3] of each of whom he says, "he was honoured like a god among the people." These words suggest a high and sacrosanct position ; yet these two priests are also warriors fighting in the ranks, which is the mark of a secular priesthood ; and there is no legend nor any hint of evidence suggesting that a professional priesthood enjoyed a political and social power in the prehistoric that we know was never achieved by them in the historic period of Greece. For the evolution of many of the earliest Hellenic institutions evidence is almost wholly lacking. But on general comparative grounds we can surmise that the religious character of the monarchy was most prominent in the earliest times and that as its secular power and functions developed, the priest-expert was attached to him to assist in the national cults, over which the Basileus retained a general supervision. We have scarcely a hint, either in the earliest or later days of Greece, of any conflict between Church and State ; we know that, at least, historic Greece escaped sacerdotalism ;

[1] *Il.*, 16, 234. [2] *Il.*, 16, 605. [3] *Il.*, 5, 77.

and its earliest societies, whatever their danger or
their struggles may have been, had escaped it by the
days of Homer.[1] Bearing on this point is the other
negative fact, that for this earliest age we have little
or no evidence of the prevalence of what is called
' Shamanism,' divine seizures, ecstatic outbursts of
wild prophesying, by which a society can be terrified
and captured. The professional ' Mantis,' the
prophet or soothsayer, existed as distinct from the
priest ; but his methods generally—so far as our
earliest witness informs us—were cool and quasi-
scientific.[2]

The ritual at the altar in the early period with
which we are at present dealing consisted of an
oblation to the deity of an animal victim or an
offering of fruits and cereals ; the sacrifice might be
accompanied with wine or might be wineless, a
' sober ' sacrifice which was called νηφάλια, the
latter being perhaps the more ancient tradition. We
may interpret the earliest form of Hellenic animal-
sacrifice as in some sense a simple tribal or family
communion-meal with the deity, whereby the sense
of comradeship and clan-feeling between man and
God was strengthened and nourished. This is the
view that Homer has inherited, and it endures
throughout the later history of the ritual ; and it
expresses the general genial temper of Hellenic
religion, a trait which Robertson Smith marked as
characteristic of other religions of the same social
type.[3] Similarly the description given us by Theophrastos and Pausanias of the ancient ritual of Zeus

[1] He is aware, however, that a θεοῦ ὀμφή, an oracular mandate, might be delivered against the royal house. *Od.*, 3, 215.
[2] Vide my *Cults*, 4, p. 190.
[3] *Religion of the Semites*, pp. 236–245.

Polieus on the Athenian Akropolis reveals to us a typical example of the civic communion feast.[1] Such a sacrifice is merely a transference into the divine circle of the practice of the common feast of the tribesmen. But we can also discern a mystic element in the Homeric ritual text, which is evidently based on a tradition indefinitely older than the poems ; the sacrificial victim, usually the ox, is first consecrated by being touched with the barley-stalks, which had been placed on the altar and which fill him by their contact with the altar's divine spirit : then when he has been immolated and cut up, the sacrificers are specially said " to taste the entrails "[2] invariably before the real sacred meal begins ; as the entrails are the inner seat of the life which has been consecrated by the hallowing contact of the altar, we are justified in supposing that the object of this solemn act was to establish the real and corporeal communion of the worshipper with the divinity.[2]

Chthonian worship.—The important distinction which is well attested of the later ages between the ' chthonian ' and the ' Olympian ' ritual—to use these two conventional terms for convenience— may already have been in vogue in the earliest period of the polytheism. In the first type of sacrifice, where the offering was made to the nether divinities, the victim's head was held down above a hole in the ground—a βόθρος—and the blood from the severed throat was shed into it. In the second, where the upper powers, whose region was the air or

---

[1] Vide *Cults*, 1, pp. 88–92.
[2] Vide my *Greece and Babylon*, p. 236; also my article on " Sacrificial Communion in Greek Religion " in *Hibbert Journal*, 1904 : on " Sacrifice " (Greek), in Hastings' *Encyclopœdia of Religion and Ethics*.

the sky, were the recipients, the victim was held up
erect off the ground, his face lifted towards the sky,
and in this attitude his throat was cut. Homer
shows himself aware of this form of sacrifice ; and
that the other, the chthonian, was also in vogue in
his time is to be inferred from his account of the
ritual performed by Odysseus in honour of the
shades, where he mentions the βόθρος, the sacrifice of
black sheep, with their heads turned downwards
towards the lower world, and the triple libation of
honey, wine and water.[1] For the ritual of the dead
in the Greek religious tradition was closely modelled
on the service of the nether divinities. The triple
libation is known to have been part of Minoan-
Cretan cult, as the altar table found in the cave of
Mount Dikte attests.[2] And a shrine with a βόθρος
in the middle of the cella has been found at Priniá
in Crete, consecrated to a chthonian goddess, of
which the foundation is ascribed to the ninth
century.[3]

From these indications and from the prevalence
of chthonian cults attested by later records, in
which we can discern features of great antiquity, we
can gather that the earliest period of Greek religion
was not wholly characterised by the brightness of
ritual and the geniality of religious feeling that
appear on the surface of Homeric poetry. The
Homeric sacrifice was often accompanied by a sense
of sin,[4] though the poet shows no cognisance of any
peculiar ritual of a specially piacular type. Also he
was aware of the dark world of powers who avenged

[1] *Od.*, 10, 517–520, 528.
[2] Vide Evans' " Mycenæan Tree and Pillar Cult," *Hell. Journ.*,
901, p. 191.
[3] *Arch. Anzeig.*, 1909, p. 98.   [4] e.g. *Il.*, 9, 500.

the broken oath and punished sinners even after death. Long before his time, we may suppose, gloomy worship, such as that of the Θεοὶ Μειλίχιοι described by Pausanias at Myonia in Lokris,[1] of which the rites were performed by night, was in vogue in parts of Greece. Mother-Earth, prophesying through phantom-dreams, had held rule at Delphi before Apollo came, and that was long before Homer's work began.[2]

There are strong reasons also for believing that the cult of hero-ancestors was already a part of the pre-Homeric religion, as it was a prominent part of the post-Homeric. The elaborate tendance of the dead attested of the Mycenæan period by the graves discovered at Tiryns and Mycenæ, could easily develop into actual worship if it was maintained through many generations, as it was at Menidi in Attica. Doubtless, the common and promiscuous worship of the dead was a morbid development of the later polytheism. But Homer, who is generally silent about such cults, and in a well-known passage about the Twin-Brethren[3] seems to ignore deliberately their divine or semi-divine character, almost reveals his knowledge of the worship of Herakles,[4] and certainly was aware of the Attic cult of Erechtheus, unless the passage that refers to it was the work of the interpolator.[5]

It is a difficult question how we are to estimate and how far we can trust the Homeric evidence on this important point of religion. Even if we trust it so far as to say that the Achæans at least practised

---

[1] 10, 38, 8. [2] *Cults*, 4, pp. 180, 193.
[3] *Il.*, 3, 243 : but the poet of the Nekyia is well aware of the heroic or divine honours paid them, *Od.*, 11, 300–304.
[4] *Od.*, 11, 602. [5] *Il.*, 2, 548.

no real worship of the dead, it yet remains probable that they found it existing here and there in the lands in which they settled.

It is important to emphasise this gloomier side of Greek religion ; but it is detrimental to exaggerate it, as has been the tendency of some modern writers in a pardonable revolt from the old shallow theories of orthodox classicism. We ought to recognise that at no period of his history was the ordinary Hellene ghost-ridden, worried and dismayed by demoniac terrors, or by morbid anxiety about the other world or his destiny after death ; at least he will not appear so, when we compare his religious and mythologic records with those of Babylon, Egypt, and Christendom.[1] Nor dare we affirm that the prehistoric Hellene was weaker-minded and more timorous in respect of such matters than the later. He may even have been stronger-minded, and at least as willing to eat a sacramental meal in company with the ' Theoi Meilichioi ' (shadowy powers of the lower world), or with the Nether-Zeus, or the Nether Earth-Mother, and with his departed family-spirits, as were his later descendants at Lokris, Mykonos and other places.[2] The earliest myths have little of the goblin element. Homer indeed himself was cognisant of such forms of terror as a black ' Ker '—Penelope likens Antinoos to one ;[3] the ancient folklore of Argolis was aware of a bad spirit that once ravaged its homes.[4] The early popular imagination was sure to have inherited or to have evolved such creations of fear ; and a black Earth-Goddess with a horse's

---

[1] Vide *Greece and Babylon*, pp. 206–207.
[2] Vide v. Prott, *Leges Græcorum Sacræ*, n. 4. Cf. *Arch. für Religionsw.*, 1909, pp. 467, 482–485.
[3] *Od.*, 17, 500.   [4] Paus., 1, 43, 7.

head and snake-locks, who lived in a dark cave at
Phigaleia, almost certainly in the pre-Homeric
period, was a sufficiently terrifying personality.[1]

But happily for the Greek imagination, the
divinities of the world of death, abiding below the
earth, tended to take on the benign functions of the
powers of vegetation. The God of the lower world
is scarcely called by the ill-omened name of Hades
in cult, but Plouton or Trophonios or Zeus Chthonios,
names importing beneficence ; for the Homeric and
Hesiodic world Demeter is a goddess of blessing, not
of terror. And although in the earliest period certain
demoniac personages such as Medousa—identical in
form and perhaps in character with the snake-locked
horse-headed Demeter—may have loomed large and
terrible in popular cult, and afterwards faded wholly
from actual worship or survived in the lower strata
of ineffectual folklore, yet the more civilising
imagination had also been operative in the religion
of the second millennium. The monuments of the
Minoan-Mycenæan religion reveal scarcely an element of terror. And at some period before Homer
the kindly deity, Hermes, had assumed the function
of the leader of souls. As regards the eschatological
views of the prehistoric Greek we can say little,
unless we believe that Homer was his spokesman ;
and such belief would be very hazardous. The
earliest communities may have had no special hopes
concerning the departed soul ; we have no reason
for thinking that the mysteries which came to offer
some promise of happiness in the world to come had
as yet proclaimed such a doctrine ; the earliest form
of the Eleusinia may have been that of a secret

[1] *Cults*, 3, pp. 50–62.

society organised for agrarian purposes. But, on the other hand, there is no proof that the primitive mind of the Hellene brooded much on the problem of death, or was at all possessed with morbid feeling about it ; and in pre-Homeric times he must have been freer from care in this matter than he was in the later centuries, if we accept the view of certain scholars that the elaborate ritual of ' Katharsis ' or purification, which was mainly dependent on the idea of the impurity of death, ghosts and bloodshed, was wholly the creation of post-Homeric days.

Earliest ritual of purification.—It has been even said that the very idea of the need of purification on special occasions was unknown to Homer. This is demonstrably false ; it is enough to mention one passage alone : at the close of the first book of the *Iliad*, the Achæans at Agamemnon's bidding, purify themselves from the plague, and throw the infected media of purification into the sea ; this is a religious lustration. And when Hesiod mentions the rule that a man returning from an ' ill-omened ' funeral could not without peril attempt to beget a child on that day,[1] he happens to be the first literary witness to the Greek tabu of death ; but we may be sure that he is giving us a tradition of indefinite age, and that the ' Achæan ' society, of which Homer is supposed to be the spokesman, had some of the Kathartic rules and superstitions that are found broadcast in later Greece. It may not have elaborated or laid marked stress on them ; it may have had no strong sense of the impurity of homicide nor devised any special code for its expiation. But if it was entirely without any instinctive feeling for the

[1] *Op.*, 735.

impurity of birth and death, and for the danger of
the 'miasma' arising from certain acts and states,
it was almost unique among the races of man. Only,
a progressive people does not overstrain such
feelings.

Such a religion as has been sketched might accord
with a high social and political morality. On the
other hand, it would not be likely to foster
and consecrate certain mental moods, ennobled by
Christian ethic, such as 'fear of God,' humility,
faith. Never in the free periods of Greek history was
'deisidaimonia' ('fear of divine powers') regarded
as a virtue, but rather as a vice or weakness. The
Hellene was humble in his attitude to God only in
the sense that he disliked overweening acts and
speech of self-glorification; the phrase, δοῦλος
τοῦ θεοῦ, 'slave of God,' common in early Christian documents, would be as repugnant to the
Hellene as would be the ecstasy of self-abasement
congenial to the Babylonian and the Christian
religions. As for the Pauline use of the word πίστις,
'faith,' its value for religious morality would have
been unintelligible for the earlier Greek.[1]

Cruder religious conceptions in the earliest period.—
So far, the religious phenomena discoverable with
some certainty or some probability in the earliest
period of Greek history indicate a theistic system
of a somewhat advanced type. But doubtless we
must reckon with the presence of much else that
was cruder and more savage. When we find in the
later records ample evidence of the lower products
of the religious imagination, the products of 'animism' or 'fetichism' or 'theriomorphism' or 'poly-

----

[1] Vide my *Greece and Babylon*, pp. 192–194.

daimonism,' more inarticulate and uncouth embodiments of the concept of divinity, or darker and more cruel ritual than that which Homer describes, such as human sacrifice, the driving out of the scapegoat, blood-magic for controlling winds or finding water, no reasonable critic will call all these things post-Homeric because they may not be mentioned in Homer, or suppose that the pure-minded Hellenes were seduced into borrowing them from the Orientals, or that they were spontaneous products of a later degenerate age. The view taken of them by those who have in recent times applied comparative Anthropology to the study of Hellenism is the only one that is possible on the whole ; these things are a surviving tradition of a mode of religious thought and feeling proper to the aboriginal ancestors of the Hellenic race, or immemorial indigenous products of the soil upon which that race grew up. There is no cataclysm in the religious history of Greece, no violent breach with its past, no destruction of primitive forms at the advent of a higher enlightenment ; no fanatic prophet arose, and the protests of philosophy were comparatively gentle and ineffective. Only a few religious forms of an undeveloped society that might shock a more civilised conscience were gradually abandoned ; most of them were tolerated, some in a moribund condition, under a more advanced religion, with which they might be seen to clash if any one cared to reason about them. Therefore a chapter or a statement in Pausanias may really be a record of the pre-Homeric age ; and in this way we can supplement the partial picture that has been given above.

Animal-Gods and Animal-worship.—The anthro-

pomorphic principle, which is not necessarily the
highest upon which a personal theism could be constructed, is the main force of the higher life of
Hellenic polytheism. We may believe that it had
begun to work before Homer, but not predominantly
or with sufficient effect to produce a stable anthropomorphism in religion. Some worship of animals
which is called 'theriolatry,' some beliefs in the
animal-incarnations of the divinity, were certainly
in vogue. A few of the more ancient cult-titles would
be evidence sufficient, apart from the later records.
One of the most significant and oldest is Λύκειος,
an epithet of Apollo marking his association with
wolves ; we find also that in many legends and even
occasionally in ritual the wolf appears as his sacred
animal. These facts point back to a period when
Apollo was still the hunter-god of the wild wood, and
was regarded as occasionally incarnate in the beast
of the wild. We have also a few indications of
direct reverence being paid to the wolf, apart from
its connection with any god.[1] Another salient
example either of theriolatry or theriomorphic god-
cult is snake-worship, proved to have existed in the
earliest epoch of the Delphic religion, and in vogue
according to later records in Epirus and Macedonia.
It may have been reverenced in its own right, or as
the incarnation of some personal divinity or hero, as
we find it later attached to the chthonian deities, to
the Earth-Mother, Zeus Κτήσιος and Μειλίχιος,[2]
Asklepios, and to the buried hero or heroine, such as
Erechtheus, Kychreus. We have also reasons for
assuming a very early cult of a Bear-Artemis in

[1] *Cults*, 4, pp. 113–116.
[2] Vide Nilsson, in *Athen. Mitth.*, 1908, p. 279.

Attica[1] and Arcadia ; and many other examples of similar phenomena will be found in a treatise on the subject by De Visser.[2] Later Arcadia was full of the products and of the tradition of this early mode of religious imagination ; besides the horse-headed Demeter at Thigaleia, we hear of the worship at the same place of a goddess called Eurynome, represented as half-woman, half-fish ; and bronze figures, belonging to the Roman period, have been found at Lykosoura in Arcadia, apparently representations of divinities partly theriomorphic.[3]

The first anthropologists who dealt with the primitive forms of Hellenic religion read this special set of phenomena in the light of totemism ; but progressive students have now abandoned the totemistic hypothesis, on the ground that there is little or no trace of Totemism in any Greek or any Aryan Society, and that theriolatry, or the direct worship of animals, needs no such explanation. Also, as I have recently pointed out elsewhere,[4] the theriomorphic concept of divinity can and frequently does co-exist at certain periods and in certain peoples with the anthropomorphic ; nor can we say with assurance that in the mental history of our race the former is prior to the latter, or that generally the anthropomorphic was evolved from the animal-god.

Functional Deities : polydæmonism.—In attempting to penetrate the pre-Homeric past, we have to reckon with another phenomenon which, though

---

[1] *Cults*, 2, pp. 434–449.

[2] *De Græcorum deis non referentibus speciem humanam*, 1900.

[3] *Bull. Corresp. Hellén.*, 1899, p. 635.

[4] *Greece and Babylon*, pp. 66–80. Vide Schrader's article, " Aryan Religion," Hastings' *Encyclopædia*, vol. 2, p. 38.

revealed in later records only, has certainly a primitive character and has been regarded as belonging to an age when the concept of definite complex personalities, such as θεοί, had not yet arisen. It was Usener[1] who first called attention to a large number of local cults of personages unknown to myth or general literature and designated, not by what are called proper names, such as Hermes, Apollo, Zeus, but by transparent adjectival names, expressing a particular quality or function or activity, to which the essence of the divine power in each case was limited : such, for instance, are Ἔχετλος Ἐχετλαῖος ἥρως, Κυαμίτης, Εὔνοστος, being nothing more, respectively, than the hero of the ploughshare at Marathon, the ' hero who makes the beans grow' on the sacred way to Eleusis, ' the hero who gives the good return of corn ' at Tanagra ; for these he invented the term, ' Sonder-Götter,' meaning deities of a single function only ; and to those of them to whom only a momentary function and therefore only a momentary existence seemed to appertain, he applied the term ' Augenblick-Götter,' ' Momentary Gods ' ; an Hellenic example of this type might be ' Μυίαγρος,' ' Fly-chaser,' in Arcadia, and Elis, who at the sacrifice to Athena or Zeus was called upon to chase away the flies that would worry the sacrificers, and who only existed for the purpose and at the time of that call.

We may compare also, for vagueness and inchoateness of personality, certain aggregates of deities having no definite single existence, but grouped by some adjectival functional name, such as θεοὶ Ἀποτρόπαιοι, ' the deities that avert evil,' at Sikyon,[2]

---

[1] *Götternamen*, 1896.   [2] Paus., 2, 11, 2.

θεαὶ Γενετυλλίδες, the goddesses of birth, in Attica,[1]
the θεαὶ Πραξιδίκαι, the goddesses of just requital,
at Haliartos.[2] Such forms seem to hover on the
confines of ' polydaimonism,' and to be the products
of an embryonic perception of divinity, cruder and
dimmer than the robust and bright creations of the
Hellenic polytheism, to which so rich a mythology
and so manifold a personality attached. And
another fact seems to fall into line with these ; in
some cult-centres the deity, though personally and
anthropomorphically conceived, might only be
designated by some vague descriptive title, like
ὁ θεός and ἡ θεά, as occasionally at Eleusis, or
' Despoina,' 'the Mistress,' the Goddess of Arcadia,
or ' Παρθένος ', the ' Virgin,' on the coast of Caria,
and in the Chersonnese ; even as late as the time of
Pausanias the men of Boulis in Phokis never called
their highest God[3] by any other name than ὁ
Μέγιστος, ' the Greatest.' And it has been thought
that the well-known statement of Herodotus that
the Pelasgians had no names for their divinities was
based on some such facts as these.

The importance of these phenomena would be all
the greater if Usener's theory were true that they
represent the crude material out of which much of
Greek polytheism has grown.[4] But in any case they
claim mention here, because they are the products
of a mental operation or instinct that must have

[1] Paus., 1, 1, 5.   [2] Paus., 9, 33, 3.
[3] Paus., 10, 37, 3.
[4] I have criticised this theory of evolution in *Anthropological
Essays presented to E. B. Tylor*, 1907, " The place of the Sonder-
götter in Greek Polytheism," where I have taken the view that
some of them are products of the same religious instinct that
produces theism or polytheism and that some appear to be late
offshoots of the polytheistic system.

been operative in the earliest period of Hellenic religion.

Animism or animatism.—In another set of facts, also attested by later records, we may discern the surviving addition of an animistic period. A large part of the Hellenic, as of other religions, reflects man's relation and feeling towards the world of nature, his dependence on the fruits of the earth, the winds, the waters, and the phenomena of the sky. The trend of the higher polytheism in the Hellenic mind was to set the personal divinity above and outside these things, which he or she directs as an intellectual will-power. But we have sufficient evidence of another point of view which is that of more primitive religion, from which the deity is imagined as essentially immanent in the thing, not as a distinct personality emerging and separable from it. The Arcadians who worshipped 'Zeus Keraunos,'[1] or 'Zeus-Thunder,' at Mantineia, or the people at Gythion in Laconia, who called a sacred meteoric stone, 'Zeus Καππώτας,'[2] 'the fallen Zeus,' or the Athenians who worshipped 'Demeter χλόη,' 'Demeter Green Verdure,'[3] reveal in these strange titles an attitude of mind that is midway between 'animatism,' that religious perception of each striking thing or phenomenon in nature as in itself mysteriously alive and divine, and 'theism' which imagines it controlled by a personal deity. At the stage when Demeter could be named and perceived as 'Chloe,' 'Verdure,' the anthropomorphic conception of divinity, though certainly existing, was not yet stable or crystallised.

---

[1] *Bull. Corr. Hell.*, 1878, p. 515.   [2] Paus., 3, 22, 1.
[3] *Id.*, 1, 22, 3 ; for other references vide *Cults*, 3, p. 312, R.9.

But there are other cult-facts reported to us of a still cruder type that seem to reveal animatism pure and simple and the infancy of the Hellenic mind. The Arcadians,[1] always the most conservative and backward among the Hellenes, in their colony of Trapezus, ' offered sacrifice to the lightning and thunder and storms ' ; it seems that for them these things were animate and divine directly, just as the Air—Bedu—was for the Macedonians. Again, through all the periods of Hellenic religion, the worship of rivers and springs only at certain points approached the borders of theism ; sometimes offerings were flung directly into the water, and prayer might be made ' into the water '—we must not say ' to the river-god,' but to the divine water.[2]

We discern these two different ways of imagining divinity in the worship and ideas attaching to Helios, ' Sun,' and Hestia, ' Hearth ' ; as regards the former, we have reason to surmise that his religious prestige was higher in the pre-Homeric than in the later age, and that the exalted position as a great political and cultured God which he enjoyed in the later history of Rhodes was a heritage from the Minoan religious tradition.[3] In Homer's poems we find him personal and anthropomorphised ; but we may well doubt if he was so for the average Greek, who merely kissed his hand to him every morning or bowed to him on coming forth from his house, and who, regarding him merely as animate, or ' Living Sun,' found it difficult to develop him

---

[1] Paus., 8, 29, 1.

[2] Paus., 8, 38, 3. ὁ ἱερεὺς τοῦ Λυκαίου Διὸς προσευξάμενος ἐς τὸ ὕδωρ. Cf. Hesiod., *Op.*, 737 ; for the general facts vide *Cults*, 5, pp. 420–424.

[3] Vide *Cults*, 5, pp. 417–420.

into a free and complex individual person. As regards Hestia the facts are still clearer.[1] In her worship, which belonged to the aboriginal period of Greek religion, she was at first, and in the main she continued to be, nothing more than ' Holy Hearth,' the Hearth felt as animate, nor was the attempt to anthropomorphise into a free personal Goddess ever wholly successful.

Magic.—Now that which is here called ' animatism ' is a religious feeling which may inspire real worship, but is more liable than pure theism to be associated with magic ; and it is reasonable to believe that magic was in vogue in prehistoric Hellas, not necessarily in antagonism to religion, but practised for purposes of the community as well as for private ends.

It is true that the records which tell us about these things are all of a period much later than Homer's, and that he is almost silent about such matters.[2] But we know now how to appreciate Homer's silences. And general anthropology compels us to believe that some of those records reveal facts of immemorial antiquity in Greece. The Thesmophoria, one of the most ancient of the Hellenic services, was partly magical ; that is, it included rites that had a direct efficacy, apart from the appeal to any divinity, such as the strewing the fields with the decaying remains of the pigs that had been consecrated to the earth-Goddesses and thrown down into their vault.[3] So also in the Thargelia of

[1] Vide *Cults*, 5, pp. 345–365.
[2] Agamede of Ephyra seems to have practised harmless magic, *Il.*, 14, 740 ; and the poet may have regarded the Elean Ephyra as the special home of magic. Vide *Od.*, 2, 328.
[3] *Cults*, 3, p. 85–93 ; Miss Harrison, *Prolegomena,* pp. 120–136

Attica and other Greek communities, the ceremonies connected with the scapegoat, the ritualistic whipping and transference of sin, belong to the domain of magic rather than to religion.[1]

We have also direct testimony of a magical dealing with the elements in the titles of officials at Athens called the ' Heudanemoi '[2] and of those at Corinth called 'Aνεμοκοῖται,[3] both words denoting ' windlullers,' those ' who charmed the winds to sleep ' ; and again in the description of the rite performed by the magicians at Kleonai who according to Clemens[4] " averted the sky's wrath by incantations and sacrifices " ; or in Pausanias' account of the operations of the priest of the winds at Titane in Sikyon[5] who endeavoured to assuage their fierceness by " singing over them the spells that Medea used." Doubtless these officials are only maintaining the practices of an indefinitely remote past. And these are also reflected in the legend of the ancient Salmoneus of Thessalian and possibly Minyan origin, who drove about in a chariot imitating thunder and, while merely practising a well-known type of weather-magic, was misunderstood by the higher powers and later moralists.

The few records that may avail for an opinion concerning the early period with which we are at present concerned entirely fail to suggest any such prevalence of magic as might obstruct intellectual progress or the growth of a higher religion. They reveal generally a type that is harmless or even philanthropic.[6] Doubtless some black magic

---

[1] *Cults*, 4, p. 268, etc.   [2] Arrian, *Anab.*, 3, 16, 8.
[3] Hesych., *s.v.*   [4] *Strom.*, p. 755.   [5] 2, 12, 1.
[6] In the earliest versions of her legend, the magic of Media is not black but benevolent.

existed in the earliest as in the later Hellas, directed against the life or the property of individuals, and worked by evil means ; the more ancient literature is entirely silent about this ; but a late record of Pausanias testifies to a barbarous magic practised by the community of Haliartos to discover a water-supply[1] : a son of one of the chief men was stabbed by his own father, and as he ran bleeding about the land springs of water were found where his blood dripped. But at no time, we may judge, was the religion or the intellect of Greece so clouded with magic as was the case elsewhere in the ancient civilisations, notably in Egypt and Mesopotamia.

Human sacrifices.—This attempted presentation of the first era of Greek religion must raise the question as to the practice within it of the ritual of human sacrifice. For we are apt to associate this with a primitive society and with a crude or savage religion. But this association is not borne out by the religious history of mankind. The practice has been found in societies highly developed both in morality and civilisation ; and the a priori argument is dangerous, whether we apply it in one way or the other.

It has been said that the Homeric poems show no consciousness of the existence of the cruel rite in the Greek world of the period ; and it has been argued on this ground that the Achæan society of which they are the voice was innocent of it.[2] A doubt may arise concerning the slaughter of the Trojan captives at the pyre of Patroklos,[3] an act of ferocity for which Homer outspokenly blames Achilles. The passage

[1] 9, 33, 4.
[2] Andrew Lang, *The World of Homer*, pp. 210, 216.
[3] *Il.*, 23, 174.

certainly suggests that the poet was aware that such things were occasionally done at contemporary funerals ; in Mycenæan tombs at Argos and Mycenæ human remains have been found before the entrance-door that point to an offering of slaves or captives.[1] But this need not have been an act of worship or strictly of religion. The dead might be imagined as needing slaves ; and to kill slaves to accompany the departed, just as to kill horses over the pyre, may only imply ' tendance ' and no worship of the spirit. But Homer's silence concerning human sacrifice as a rite of religion is of no value as evidence for our present question, as I have argued elsewhere.[2] How are we to account for the fairly numerous records of actual human sacrifice, or of the semblance or reminiscence of it, in later Greek worship, records that are found sporadically among most of the leading Greek stocks ? The old shift of attributing to Oriental influences everything in Hellenic religion that clashed with our ideal of Hellenism was naïvely unscientific. That the practice should have sprung up spontaneously and suddenly in the later society, when civic life and morality were advancing, is hard to believe. It is more natural to suppose that it was an immemorial and enduring tradition of the race, which was only with difficulty abolished and which lingered here and there till the end of paganism. It has been found among many other Aryan races, and it was especially in vogue among the Thraco-Phrygian stock, of near kin to the Hellenic. These general grounds for believing that

[1] Vide Tsountas in *Ephem. Archaiol.*, 1888, pp. 130–131, and Vollgraff, in *Bull. Corr. Hell.*, 1904, p. 370.

[2] Vide *Hibbert Lectures*, "Higher Aspects of Greek Religion," pp. 19, 20.

it was a feature of the earliest Greek religion are confirmed by some special evidence derivable from the legends and cult-records. It is generally impossible to date the birth of legends ; but some can be discerned to belong to an earlier stratum than others ; such are the legends concerning the human sacrifice to Zeus Λύκαιος on Mount Lykaion in Arcadia, to which is attached the story of King Lykaon and the banquet that he offers to Zeus on the flesh of his own son ;[1] the Achæan or Minyan story of the sacrifice to Zeus Laphystios—Zeus the Ravening—of the king's son of the house of Athamas ;[2] Kyknos' sacrifice of pilgrims and the dedication of their skulls to Apollo on the Hyperborean pilgrims'-way at the Achæan Pagasos ;[3] the sacrifice of a boy and a maiden to Artemis Τρικλαρία by the Ionians on the southern shore of the Gulf of Corinth.[4] A careful study of the legends of these various rites will convince one that they belong to the earliest period of Greek religion. The last example is specially illuminating : the human sacrifice is here practised by the Ionians in their ancient settlements in the land, afterwards called Achaia ; and its cessation is connected with the arrival of the cult of Dionysos and the return of the heroes from Troy.

The purpose and significance of the rite differed probably in the different cult-centres. In most cases we may interpret it as piacular, the dedication to an offended deity of a valued life, the life of the king's son or daughter, as a substitute for the life of the people, such vicarious sacrifice being a common human institution ; in some few cases we may

---

[1] Vide *Cults*, 1, p. 40–42.　　　　[2] *Ib.*, p. 42.
[3] *Ib.*, 4, p. 272 ; Schol. Pind., *Ol.*, 10, 19.　　[4] 7, 19, 1–9.

discern an agricultural motive, the blood being shed as a magic charm to secure fertility.[1] At certain cult-centres and at certain times the human victim may have been regarded as the incarnation of the deity or the ' daimon ' ; and this idea might explain the legends concerning the slaying of Iphigeneia the priestess of Artemis, or of the priests of Dionysos. Finally, in the ritual of Zeus Lykaios, we may detect a cannibal-sacrament, in which the holy flesh of the victim, whose life was mystically one with the God's and the people's, was sacramentally devoured. This ghastly practice is only doubtfully disclosed by legends and by interpretation of later records ; a faint reminiscence of it may also have survived in the Argive story of Harpalyke and Klymenos.[2] But a close parallel to it will be noted in the Thracian Dionysiac ritual.

Summary account of the first period.—A detailed account of the pre-Homeric religious age must at many points remain doubtful and hypothetical ; but certain definite and important facts may be established. Anthropomorphism, in a degree not found in the earliest Roman religion, was already prevalent, even dominant ; and nearly all the leading personal divinities of the later polytheism had already emerged ; only Dionysos had not yet crossed the border from Thrace ; Asklepios, dimly known to Homer, was merely the local deity of a small Thessalian community, Pan merely the daimon of flocks in remote Arcadia. Cretan religion, also personal in its imagination and mainly anthropomorphic, had left its deep imprint on the mainland ; and its divine personalities, such as Rhea, the

---

[1] e.g. vide *Cults*, 3, 93.   [2] *Cults*, 3, p, 22.

Mother of the Gods, and Aphrodite were soon adopted by the northern immigrants, but not at first into high positions. The deity was generally imagined not as a spirit or a vague cosmic force, but as glorified man, and therefore the religion became adaptable to human progress in arts, civilisation and morality. But much in the animal world still appeared sacred and weird ; and the deity might be at times incarnate in animal form. At the same time the religious imagination was still partly free from the bias of personal theism, and produced vaguer divine forms, of some force and power, but belonging rather to ' animatism ' or polydaimonism than to polytheism.

Finally a study of all the facts and probabilities may convince a careful student that the origin of Greek polytheism as a whole from simpler forms cannot be found in this earliest period. In the second millennium, which is the starting-point for Hellenic history proper, we cannot discern the ' making of a God ' (unless we mean the building-up of his more complex character), nor do we start with a godless period. We may well believe that in the history of mankind theism was evolved from animism or polydaimonism ; we may believe the much more doubtful theory that anthropomorphism arises from a previous theriomorphism, and there may still be some who are convinced that theriomorphism implies a totemistic society. But, at any rate, these various evolutions had already happened indefinitely before the two strains—the Northern and the Mediterranean—had blended into the Hellenic race. The higher and the lower, the more complex and the simpler, forms of religious imagination operate together throughout Hellenic history ; and the higher, though dominant, never wholly absorbs the lower, both being an intellectual tradition of an indefinite past. Much work on the origins of Greek religion has been wasted because its chronology is anachronistic. And the attempt to unlock many of its mysteries by the key of totemism has been abandoned by those who recognise that many of the views concerning this social pheno-menon and its religious importance, prevalent in a former generation, were erroneous.

CHAPTER III

THE SECOND PERIOD, 900–500 B.C.

WE can now pursue the enquiry nearer the borderline of the historic period, as it is conventionally termed.

Introduction of worship of Dionysos.—As early as the tenth century B.C., and probably earlier, a new religion with a new and imposing divinity was intruding itself into Hellenic lands from Thrace and Macedonia.[1] Dionysos and the Thracian ritual-legend of Lykourgos are known to Homer ; but the poems suggest that he was not yet definitely received into the Hellenic pantheon. Yet there are reasons for believing that Bœotia had received the alien worship in the 'Minyan' epoch, before the incoming of the 'Boiotoi'; and Attica before the Ionic emigration; while in the Peloponnese the Argive legend associates the advent of the god with the names of Perseus and the Prœtid dynasty. In spite of local opposition and its natural antagonism to the nascent spirit of Hellenism, which was now tending to express itself in certain definite and orderly forms of mood, thought and feeling, the new religion won its way victoriously, taking Thebes for its Hellenic metropolis, and some time afterwards securing its position at Delphi, where the priesthood and the Apolline oracle become its eager champions.

---

[1] Vide *Cults*, vol. 5, pp. 85–118. Cf. generally chs. iv and v.

It was distinguished from the traditional Hellenic in regard to its idea of divine personality, its ritual and its psychic influence, that is to say, the mood that it evoked in the votary. In the first place, the figure of Dionysos belonged indeed to personal theism, certainly in Hellenic cult and probably in the Thracian ; but he was less sharply defined as a concrete individual than was, for instance, Apollo or Athena ; he was vaguer in outline, a changeful power conceived more in accordance with daimon-istic, later with pantheistic thought, incarnate in many animal-shapes and operative in the life-processes of the vegetative world ; and an atmosphere of nature-magic accompanied him.

The central motives of his oldest form of ritual were the birth and death of the God, a conception pregnant of ideas that were to develop in the religious future, but alien to the ordinary Hellenic theology, though probably not unfamiliar to the earlier Cretan-Mycenæan creed. But the death of this God was partly a fact of ritual ; he was torn to pieces by his mad worshippers and devoured sacra-mentally, for the bull or the goat or the boy whom they rent and devoured was supposed to be his temporary incarnation, so that by this savage and at times cannibalistic communion they were filled with his blood and his spirit and acquired miraculous powers. By such an act and—we may suppose—by the occasional use of intoxicants and other nervous stimulants the psychic condition that this worship evoked was frenzy and ecstasy, which might show itself in wild outburst of mental and physical force, and the enthusiastic feeling of self-abandonment in which the worshipper escaped the limits of his own nature and achieved a temporary sense of identity with the God ; and such union with divinity might avail him even after death. This privilege of ecstasy might be used for the practical purposes of vegetation-magic, yet was desired and proclaimed for its own sake, as a more intense mood of life. This religion preached no morality and could ill adapt itself to civic life ; its ideal was supranormal psychic energy. The process whereby it was half captured and half tamed by the young Hellenic spirit forms one of the most interesting chapters in Hellenism.

It is convenient for the purposes of religious study to mark off the period between the ninth and the sixth centuries as the second period of Greek religion, in which we can observe the working of new forces and the development of older germs into new life. By the beginning of this period the fusion of the Northerners and the Mediterranean population was mainly complete, and the Hellenic spirit had acquired its definite instincts and bias. The ninth and the eighth centuries witnessed the diffusion of epic literature, the rise of lyric poetry, the emergence of the ' eikon ' or idol in religious art, and generally the development of cities and civic life ; and it is essential to estimate the religious influence of these forces.

Influence of epic and lyric poetry.—That the contribution of Homeric and of the later Hesiodic literature to the shaping and fixing of Hellenic religion was most fruitful and effective cannot be doubted. Only we must not accept the exaggerating view of Herodotus[1] that these two poets were really

[1] 2, 53.

the founders of the anthropomorphic religion, creating the orthodox Hellenic theogony and determining the names and functions and shapes of the special divinities. By such a statement some scholars have been misled into regarding the Homeric poems as a kind of Greek Bible, which in respect to religious matters it might be heresy to disbelieve. But we know that local temple-legend and local folklore could always maintain its independence of Homeric, or Hesiodic authority, in respect to the titles of the Gods, their relationships and genealogies. Artemis was not everywhere reputed to have the same parentage or Zeus the same spouse. The early epic poets gathered many of the ἱεροὶ λόγοι of shrines, but there was much that they did not gather and which yet survived. There was a noticeable particularism in Greek theology, and no orthodoxy and no heterodoxy in the sense that it was moral to believe or immoral to disbelieve any sacred book.

The chief religious achievement of Homer and his fellows was to intensify the anthropomorphic trend in Greek religion, to sharpen and individualise the concepts of divinity, and to diffuse throughout the Hellenic world a certain uniformity of religious imagination. To their work partly, as well as to the higher synthetic power of the Greek mind, we may ascribe the fact that in spite of local varieties of myth and cult-title, in spite of the various elements that the divine personality may have absorbed from earlier cult-figures and cult-forms in the various cult-centres, yet the sense of the individual unity of person was not lost so long as the same name was in vogue ; hence Apollo Lykeios of Argos could not be a different person from the Apollo Patroös of Athens, nor could hostility arise between them. That is to say, the higher religious literature imprinted a certain precision and definiteness upon the personal names of the leading divinities and endowed them with a certain essential connotation ; for example, the dogma of the virginity of Athena and Artemis, always presented in the higher poetry, prevailed so far as to suppress the maternal character that may have attached to them in the prehistoric period and of which we can still discern a glimmering in certain local cults.[1] And to this task of shaping the divine characters the rising lyric poetry, which was growing up with the decay of the epic, and which in obedience to the Hellenic passion for disciplined form was developing fixed types of song and music appropriate to special festivals and worships, must have contributed much. The ' spondaic ' metre was adapted to the invocation or hymn sung at the libation—the σπονδή—to Zeus, and the solemn gravity of the spondaic fragment attributed to Terpander fittingly expresses the majesty of the high God, " the primal cause of all things, the Leader of the world."[2] The pæan and the ' nomos ' became instinct with the Apolline, the Dithyrambos with the Dionysiac spirit,[3] the spirit of order and self-restraint on the one hand, the spirit of ecstasy and passion on the other. The earlier Greek lyric was in fact mainly religious, being composed for public or private occasions of worship ; its vogue was therefore wide and in some communities, as in Arcadia, the singing

---

[1] Vide *Cults*, 2, pp. 442–449.
[2] Bergk, *Pœtœ Lyrici Grœci*, vol. III, Fr. 1.
[3] Philochoros Frag., 21, Müller, F. H. G., vol. i.

of these compositions formed part of the national training of the young.[1]

Idolatry.—Another phenomenon of importance at the beginning of this second period is the rise of idolatry, the prevalence of the use of the ' eikon ' in actual worship in place of the older aniconic ' agalma,' which had sufficed for the Minoan and the Homeric world as a token of the divine presence or as a magnet attracting it to the worshipper. This important change in the object of cult may have been beginning in the tenth century, for we have one indication of it in the Homeric poems, and recently on one of a series of vases of the early geometric style found in a grave near Knossos of the post-Minoan period the figures of an armed God and Goddess are depicted on low bases, evidently idols, and perhaps the earliest surviving of any Hellenic divinity.[2] Henceforth, although the old fetich-object, the aniconic ' agalma,' lingered long in certain shrines and holy places, the impulse towards idolatry became imperious and almost universal, exercising a mighty influence on the religious sentiment of the Hellenes both before and after the triumph of Christianity. The worship before the idol intensified the already powerful anthropo-morphic instinct of the polytheism ; and was at once a source of strength and a cause of narrowness. It brought to the people a strong conviction of the real presence of the concrete and individual divinity ; and, as it gave its mandate to the greatest art of the world, it evolved the ideal of divinity as the ideal of humanity, expressible in forms of beauty, strength, and majesty. On the other hand, it was a force

[1] Athenæ., p. 626 B.   [2] Vide *Arch. Anzeig*, 1908, p. 122.

working against the development of a more mystic, more immaterial religion, or of a consciousness of Godhead as an all-pervading spirit, such as might arise out of the vaguer religious perception of those half-personal ' daimones ' or ' numina,' which never wholly faded from the popular creed.

Progress of anthropomorphism.—It is interesting to mark within this second period the various effects of the now regnant anthropomorphism.

Those functional ' daimones ' mentioned above tend to leave the amorphous twilight of religious perception, in which the Roman ' Indigitamenta ' remained, and to be attracted into the stronger life of personal theism. 'Kourotrophos,' once perhaps only a vague functional power that nurtured children, becomes identified with Artemis or Ge ;[1] 'Χλόη,' 'Divine verdure,' when the cult was introduced from the Marathonian Tetrapolis to the Akropolis of Athens—if this indeed is a true account of its career, could only maintain herself as Demeter Χλόη.[2]

Again the name Ἥρως comes to be applied to even the most shadowy of these functional powers, to Μυίαγρος, the Fly-chaser, the most limited and momentary of them all, to Eunostos, the daimon of good harvest, about whom a very human tale is told, and to call them ' Heroes ' implies that they were imagined as semi-divine men who once lived on the earth. Even the most immaterial forces, some of those which mark mental phases or social conditions, such as Ἔρως Love, Φιλία Friendship, Εἰρήνη Peace, became often for the religious imagination personal individuals with human relationships ;[3] thus Eirene

---

[1] *Cults*, 3, pp. 17–18.   [2] *Ib.*, 3, pp. 33–34.
[3] *Cults*, 5, p. 443–447.

emerges almost as a real goddess with the traits of Demeter, Φιλία on a relief in the Jacobsen Collection is individualised as the mother of Zeus Philios, in defiance of the traditional theogony.[1] Others such as ' Αἰδώς ' ' Compassion ' remained in the border-land between animating forces and personal deities.

But we observe in many cases that the name itself was an obstacle to the emergence of a convincingly personal God or Goddess ; and where this is the case the personality never could play a leading part in the advanced religion. Thus Ἑστία bore a name that denoted nothing more than ' the Hearth,' con-sidered as animate and holy ; Greek anthropomorph-ism did its utmost for her, but never or rarely suc-ceeded in establishing her as a fully formed personal goddess. The same phenomenon is observable in regard to Ge, Helios and Selene ; it was easy to regard them as animate substances or powers and as such to worship them ; such worship they received throughout all periods of Greek religion, but no direction of the moral, social and spiritual progress of the race, for their names connoted so obviously substances unlike and alien to man that they could not with conviction be imagined as glorified men or women.[2] It was otherwise with such names as Apollo, Hera, Athena, which could become as real and individual as Miltiades or Themistokles ; and it is these humanised personalities that alone dominate the higher religion of Greece. The spiritual career of Demeter only began when men forgot the original meaning of her name and half forgot that she was

---

[1] Vide Furtwängler, in *Münchener Sitzungsber.*, 1897, 1, p. 401; Nillson, in *Athen. Mittheil.*, 1908, p. 284.

[2] The striking exception to this rule is the great cult of Helios at Rhodes. *Vide supra*, p. 29.

only Mother Earth. The 'Anemoi' being mere 'Winds,' were scarcely fitted for civic life ; but Boreas, having a personal name, could become a citizen and was actually worshipped as Πολίτης 'the Citizen' at Thourioi.[1] A curious and unscientific distinction that Aristophanes makes between the religions of the Hellenes and the Barbarians[2] has its justification from this point of view.

Influence of the Polis on religion.—The spirit of the Polis, the dominant influence in Greek religion throughout this second period, worked in the same direction as the anthropomorphic instinct ; giving complexity, varied individuality and an ever-growing social value to the idea of Godhead. The deities of the wild enter the ring-wall of the city and shed much of their wild character. Apollo Lykeios the Wolf-God, enters Argos and becomes the political leader of the State, in whose temple a perpetual fire was maintained, symbol of the perpetual life of the community.[3] And the advanced civic imagination tended to transform the primitive theriolatry or theriomorphic ideas that still survived. Proofs of direct animal worship in the later period are very rare and generally doubtful ; for the ancient writers apply the term 'worship' carelessly, applying it to any trivial act of reverential treatment.[4] In the few cases where we can still discern the animal receiving cult, we find the anomaly explained away by some association established between the animal and the anthropomorphic deity or hero. Thus the wolf became no longer sacred in

[1] Ael., *Var. Hist.*, 12, 61.
[2] " They worship Sun and Moon, we worship real Gods such as Apollo and Hermes," *Pax*, 410.   [3] Schol. Soph., *Elec.*, 6.
[4] Vide my *Greece and Babylon*, pp. 77–80.

its own right—if indeed it ever was—but might be reverenced here and there as the occasional incarnation of Apollo or as his guide or companion.

The primitive population of the Troad may once have ' worshipped ' the field-mouse, though the authority that attests it is a late and doubtful one ; but when Apollo becomes in this region the civic guardian of the Æolians and the protector of their crops, he takes a title from the mouse (Σμινθεύς from σμινθός), and the mouse is carved at the side of the anthropomorphic image as a propitiatory hint to the rest of the species not to injure the corn, or as a hint to the God that mice needed regulating.[1]

The serpent worshipped in the cavern, or in some hole or corner of the house—vaguely, in ' Aryan ' times, as the Earth-daimon or House-genius— became interpreted as the embodiment of the ancestor Erechtheus of Athens, or Kuchreus of Salamis, or Zeus Κτήσιος, the guardian of the household possessions, or of Zeus Meilichios, the nether God. When the very human Asklepios came to Athens towards the end of the fifth century, he brought with him certain dogs who were ministers of healing ; and the Athenians offered sacrificial cakes both to the God and to his dogs who partook of his sanctity.[2] This may appear a strange imbecility ; but at all events we discern in these facts the prevalent anthropomorphism dominating and transforming what it could not abolish of the old theriolatry ; just as we see the coin-artist of Phigaleia transforming the uncouth type of the horse-headed Demeter into a beautiful human form of a goddess

---

[1] Vide *Cults*, 4, pp. 163–166.
[2] Prott-Ziehen, *Leg. Saer.*, n., 18.

wearing a necklace with a horse-hoof as its pendant.
The sacred animal never wholly died out of Hellas ;
but it could only maintain its worship by entering
the service of the human gods.

The expansion of the civic system in this second
period, due to extended colonisation and commerce,
induced a development of law and an expansion of
moral and religious ideas. One of the most vital
results of the institution of the Polis was the
widening of the idea of kinship. For in theory the
city was a congregation of kinsmen, a combination
of tribes, phratries, and families, wider or narrower
associations framed on a kin-basis ; and it gradually
evolved the belief, pregnant of legal and moral
developments, that every citizen was of kin to every
other.

In consonance with the conception of the State as
an extended family, we find certain ancient family-
cults taken over into the religion of the Polis. As the
private family was knit together by the worship of
the Hearth in the hall and of Zeus Ἑρκεῖος, ' the
God of the Garth,' in the courtyard of the house, so
the City has its common Hestia or Holy Hearth,
upon which often a perpetual fire was maintained in
its ' Prytaneion ' or Common Hall ; and the Cult of
Zeus Ἑρκεῖος was established in ancient days on the
Akropolis of Athens. The organisation of the
' phratries ' was consecrated to the high deities, Zeus
Athena and—among some Ionic communities—to
Aphrodite ; and the decisions of the ' phrateres ' or
' Brothers ' on questions of adoption and legitimacy
of citizens were delivered from the altar of Zeus
Phratrios ; while the union of the local districts or
' demes ' was sanctified by the cult of Zeus or

Aphrodite Pandemos, the God or Goddess of 'all
the demes.' Also, the Polis organised and maintained the kindred-festivals of commemoration
proper to the family or gens or phratria, the All-
Souls celebration of the dead which was held at the
end of the Anthesteria ; the γενέσια, the funeral
feasts of the γένη ; the 'Apatouria,' the joint
festival of the phratries ; while the great achievement of the consolidation of the scattered groups
into the single city was celebrated at Athens by the
festival of the Συνοικέσια, the 'Union of all the
Houses,' and the Panathenaia, the all-Attic feast of
Athena.

The picture that these facts present of a State-
religion based on the idea of the family and of kinship is mainly drawn from Athens, of which the
religious record is always the richest ; but it reflects
undoubtedly the system of the other Hellenic
states as well. Many of their records attest the
belief that some one of the high divinities was the
ancestor or ancestress of the whole people, and this
ancestry was understood in the physical and literal
sense. Thus Apollo 'Patroös' was the divine
ancestor, being the father of Ion, of the Ionic
population of Attica, and even the non-Ionic stock
of that community, desired for political purposes to
affiliate themselves to this God.[1] In the same sense
he was called Γενέτωρ, 'the Father' in Delos.[2] Zeus
was the father of Arkas, the eponymous hero of the
Arcadians, and was worshipped as Πατρῷος at
Tegea [3] ; Hermes also was ancestral God of part of

[1] Plat., *Euthyd.*, p. 302 C ; Demosth., 18, § 141, 57, § 54, 67 ;
Arist., *Ath. Polit.*, 55.
[2] Diog. Laert., 8, 1, 13 ; Macrob., 3, 6, 2.
[3] *Bull. Corr. Hell.*, 1893, p. 24.

the Arcadian land and identified with the ancestor
Aipytos.[1] These religious fictions came to exert an
important influence on morality and also to develop
a certain spiritual significance which will be considered later.

Hero-cult.—This aspect of the public religion is
further emphasised by the prevailing custom of
hero-worship which appears to have gathered
strength in this second period. The hero in the
technical sense was one whose tomb was honoured
with semi-divine rites and who was regarded either
as a glorious man of the past or as the mortal
ancestor of the State or the tribe or the clan. The
first clear evidence of this in literature is in the poem
of Arktinos of Miletos called the ' Aithiopis,' that
may belong to the end of the eighth century, in
which the apotheosis of Achilles was described. But
there is, as has been said, strong reason for believing
that the practice of ' heroising ' the dead descended
from the pre-Homeric age. Nevertheless, of the
multitude of hero and ancestor cults recorded in
ancient Hellas, the greater number are probably
post-Homeric. We find the Delphic oracle giving
vigorous encouragement to the institution of them,
and in the sixth century cities begin to negotiate and
dispute about the possession of the relics of heroes.
Some of these in the older cults may have been
actual living men, dimly remembered, some were
fictitious ancestors, like Arkas and Lakedaimon,
some may have been faded deities, such as were
Eubouleus at Eleusis and Trophonios at Lebadeia.
But all were imagined by the worshipper to have
been once men or women living upon the earth. This,

[1] Paus., 8, 47, 4.

then, becomes a fact of importance for the religious thought of the world, for it engenders, or at least encourages, the belief that human beings might through exceptional merit be exalted after death to a condition of blessed immortality, not as mere spirits, but as beings with glorified body and soul. Furthermore, certain ancient heroes, long endeared to the people as the primeval parent or the war-leader of their forefathers, become raised to the position of the high God and merged in his being ; Erechtheus shares the altar and even the title of Poseidon and Zeus, Aipytos of Arcadia becomes Hermes, Agamemnon in Laconia at last is fused with Zeus.[1]

Nor in this second period were such heroic honours reserved for the remote ancestor or the great king or warrior of old, but were sometimes paid to the recently dead, to the men who had served the State well by arms or by counsel. On the assumption that Lykourgos of Sparta was a real man—and no other theory that bears scrutiny has been put forward about him—his case is the earliest recorded instance of the ' heroising ' of a personage of the historic period. A great stimulus about this time was given to this practice by the expansion of Greek colonisation, the greatest world-event of the period, which reacted in many ways on religion. As the new colonists could not take with them the tombs or the bones of the aboriginal hero of their stock, they must institute a new hero-cult, so as to bind the new citizens together by the tie of heroic kinship. The

[1] The other view, still held by some, that Zeus-Agamemnon is the earlier fact, and Agamemnon the hero the later, does not bear criticism.

most natural person to select for this high honour
was the founder or leader of the colony, the κτίστης
or ἀρχηγέτης as he was called ; and we may regard
it as the usual rule that, when he died, he would be
buried within the city and his tomb would become a
' ἡρῶον ' and would be visited yearly with annual
offerings.

That the ordinary head of the private household in
this period received posthumous honours amounting
to actual worship cannot be definitely proved. The
tendance of the dead had become indeed a matter of
religion, and at Athens was attached to the ritual of
the state by the commemorative feast of All Souls,
the χύτροι, or ' Feast of Pots,' the last day of the
Anthesteria. But nothing that is recorded of this
ghost-ceremony convicts it of actual worship ; the
ghosts are invited to spend the day with the household that holds them in affection ; they are offered
pots of porridge, and then at sunset are requested or
commanded to depart. Prayers are proffered in
their behalf to the powers of death, but not directly
to the ghosts themselves ; no cult is offered them as
to superior beings endowed with supernatural power
over the lives of individuals and states.[1] Nevertheless, the passionate service of lamentation and
the extravagant dedication of gifts which marked
the funeral ceremonies of the eighth and seventh
centuries and which certain early legislation was
framed to check, reveals a feeling about the dead
bordering on veneration and such as might inspire
actual worship.

We may safely assume that the growing interest
of the States in hero-cult intensified the family

[1] *Cults*, v, pp. 219–221 ; J. Harrison, *Prolegomena*, ch. ii.

aspect of the State-religion ; the hero as the glorious kinsman is invited to the sacrifices of the higher deities, and to the hospitable ritual known as the 'theoxenia' in which the God himself is the host.

It is important for the student of religion to mark the consequences of this close association of the civic religion with the idea of kinship that held together the family and tribe. These have been estimated more at length elsewhere[1] and only a few general observations are possible here. Where a family bond exists between the deity and the city, the spirit of genial fellowship is likely to prevail in the ritual and religious emotions, and the family meal might become the type of the public sacrificial meal with the god. Such a religion is adverse to proselytism ; for as it is the sacred prerogative of certain kindred stocks, its principle means the exclusion of the stranger. Its religious and moral feeling is naturally clannish ; the whole group must share in the moral guilt of the individual, and the sins of the fathers will be visited on the children. It affords a keen stimulus to local patriotism and quickens an ardent life within the wall of the city ; it has at the same time the natural defects of narrowness of view. Yet, in the course of religious evolution, we must regard the old Hellenic conception of the God the Father of the tribe or the city as pregnant of the larger idea of God as the Father of mankind, an idea which had already dawned upon Homer at a time when the tribal spirit of religion was still at its height.

A further result of such a system is that the

[1] Vide "Higher Aspects of Greek Religion," *Hibbert Lectures,* pp. 73–91.

State-divinities become also the patrons and guardians of the family morality, Zeus and Hera, for instance, the supervisors of the human marriage and of the duties of married life ; and copious records present the High God as the protector of the father's right ; of the tie that binds together the brethren, the sisters, the kinsmen. While such a religion was a living force, it was not likely that the family could assert itself as against the State ; to marry healthfully and early, to beget vigorous children as defenders of the State and the family graves, to cherish and honour one's parents, to protect the orphan, these were patriotic religious duties that were inspired by the developed State-religion and strenuously preached by the best ethical teachers of Greece. The State being the family 'writ large,' private morality and public could not clash. The brutal action of Kreon in the Antigone is equally an attack on the religion of the State as on that of the family ; and it was not till the fifth century that the claim of private conscience as against the family and the State could arise or that the question could be asked " Whether the good man was really the same as the good citizen."

Influence of political religion on law.—Of still greater interest is an important advance in criminal law, discernible as early as the eighth century, which may be traced partly to the growth of the City, with its extended idea of kinship, partly to the growing intensity of the belief in the power and significance of the spirits of the dead.

In the most primitive period of Hellas, the shedding of kinsman's blood was already a heinous sin ; but the slaying of one outside the kindred

circle was neither a sin against God nor a social
crime. But as the public mind of Greece became
penetrated with the feeling that all the citizens of the
Polis were in some sense akin, the slaying of a citizen
became a criminal act of which the State, and no
longer merely the clan of the slain man, would take
cognisance. And this expanded concept of law is
reflected in the expansion of an ancient and most
significant cult, the cult of Zeus Meilichios.[1] This
was the underworld God, who was angered and must
be appeased when kindred blood was shed ; as the
idea of kinship was enlarged, any civic massacre
might arouse his wrath and rites of atonement might
be offered to him. This keener sensitiveness concerning the sanctity of human life was accompanied
by a feeling that bloodshed might imprint a stain on
the slayer that rendered him ritualistically unclean,
that is, temporarily unfit to approach the Gods or
men ; it was also fortified by the growing fear of the
ghost-world, which seems to have lain more heavily
on the post-Homeric society than on Homer's men.
It is hard to give the dates for this section of the
mental history of Hellas. The first record of the
thought, which is nowhere explicit in Homer, that
homicide in certain circumstances demands purification is derived from the Aithiopis of Arktinos, the
epic poet of Miletos in the eighth century.[2] Achilles,
having slain the worthless Thersites, must retire
from the army for a while to be purified in Lesbos by
Apollo and Artemis ; we mark here that the slain
man was no kinsman of the slayer in any true sense

---

[1] Vide *Cults*, 1, pp. 64–69 ; for the religious evolution of the
Greek laws concerning homicide, vide my *Evolution of Religion*,
pp. 139–152. *Cults*, IV, pp. 295–306.

[2] *Epic. Græc. Frag.*, Kinkel, p. 33.

of the word, but was a member of the same Achæan
community, and therefore his slaying brought a
religious impurity upon the hero ; and we may
believe that the narrative reveals the early religious
law of Miletos. But we must, in passing, recognise
the possibility that these apparently new manifestations may be only a revival of immemorial thought
and feeling, common in the older non-Hellenic
societies, and only for a time suspended.[1]

Influence of Delphi and Crete.—In this post-
Homeric development of a system of purification
from bloodshed, the legends suggest that Crete and
Delphi played a momentous part. In the great
island, the cradle of European culture, the cult of
Zeus had early attached to itself certain Cathartic
ideas, probably of Dionysiac origin. And probably
in the pre-Homeric period the influence of Crete had
reached Delphi ; while the legend of the migration
of Apollo Delphinios from Crete to Delphi, and the
story that the God himself must go to this island to
be purified from the blood of Python, belong to the
second period with which we are dealing.

We have reason to believe that the Delphic God—
through the agency of his politic priesthood—was
asserting his claim in the eighth and seventh
centuries to be the dictator in the matter of purification from homicide, and thus to satisfy the cravings
of an awakening conscience. This claim may have
been suggested partly by the fear of competition with
the spreading Dionysiac religion, which also brought
with it a ' Kathartic ' message, and with which the
Delphic priesthood were wise enough to agree
quickly ; partly also by the aboriginal nature of

[1] Vide *Cults*, 4, p. 299.

Apollo, who was immemorially φοῖβος or ' pure.'
Though the claim was not universally admitted and
the Apolline jurisdiction could not obliterate the
function of other divinities in this matter, yet it was
powerful and effective of much that was vital both to
law and religion. Of the early procedure at Delphi
we know nothing. If the god exercised discretion in
his grant of purification, if he refused, for instance,
to purify the deliberate and cold-blooded murderer,
here was the opportunity for the emergence of a
civilised law of homicide. It may not have been
until the seventh century that any Hellenic state
could express in a legal establishment its consciousness of the difference between the act of murder and
the act of justifiable or accidental homicide. The
earliest that we know of was the law-court, ἐπί
Δελφινίῳ, "near the image [or shrine] of the
Dolphin-God "—established at Athens under the
patronage of the Cretan-Delphic God to try cases
where the homicide was admitted and justification
was pleaded. In this, as in other Attic courts that
dealt with the same offence, rites of purification were
often an essential adjunct of the ceremony. The
typical legend that enshrines the early ideas of
' Katharsis ' and turns on the question of justifiable
homicide is the legend of Orestes, which had spread
around the Peloponnese and penetrated Attica as
early as the eighth century, and later became Pan-
Hellenic. Apollo, as a divine agent, appears in it
first, as far as we have any literary record, in the
lyric of Stesichoros, and at some indeterminate date
in this period undertook the purification of the
matricide.

Influence of Delphi on colonisation.—These

Cathartic functions and the general demand for their exercise must have greatly enhanced the influence of Delphi in the earlier part of the post-Homeric period. It was doubtless strengthened even more by the great secular movement of Greek colonisation. With wise foresight the God had undertaken the guidance and encouragement of this already in the earliest days when the Hellenes were pushing across the sea ; for it seems as if the first Greek settlements on the Asia Minor coast, the Lycian and the Æolic, were due to his leadership if not to his inspiration. The legends that associate him with the Dorian migration into the Peloponnese are too powerful to be rejected. And after this event, when light begins to shine on Greek history and the Hellenic race was rapidly establishing that chain of colonies across and around the Mediterranean which were to diffuse Greek culture through the world, the power of Delphi and the Delphic oracle reached its zenith. For it is clear that it was the prevailing fashion to consult the Pythian Apollo as to the choice of a site. Hence it came about that in so many Greek cities Apollo was worshipped as Ἀρχηγέτης, that is, as the divine founder, and that the flourishing communities of the West sent back tithe-offerings to his shrine.[1] Was it by some accident or by something essential in his early cult and character that the God was able to play this momentous political part, such as no other deity has ever played in the secular history of his people ? The cause may lie far back in the dim antiquity of the Apolline cult, when he was specially Ἀγυιεύς, a god ‘ of the road,’ the leader of the migratory host. And

[1] Vide *Cults*, IV, pp. 200–202.

in pre-Homeric times, if not aboriginally, he was already an oracular God ; nor was any occasion so urgent for a consultation of the local oracle as when the people were setting forth on their perilous path to find a new home.[1]

The Delphic oracle.—The spiritual history of the Hellenic race in the early history period, when we mark a growing consciousness of nationality and of kinship in the various stocks, is very much a record of the career and activity of the Delphic oracle ; and this is too complex and lengthy a theme to be more than adumbrated here.[2] Due partly to the local position and the immemorial sanctity of the oracle, partly to the devotion and the grateful remembrance of the powerful Dorian states in the Peloponnese, the Pythian worship came to overshadow the Delian, and provided the chief religious centre and the strongest bond of spiritual unity in the Hellenic world. For political unity it could do little, owing to the centrifugal bias of Greek politics ; yet the Delphic Amphiktyony, the most powerful of these religious confederations that are recorded here and there in the early history of Greece, contained within it the germs of intertribal morality and concord. Its members were not indeed pledged to perpetual amity, but at least to a certain mutual forbearance even in their warlike dealings with one another. But the chief regulative functions of the oracle were concerned with questions of the institution and administration of cults, with the domains of legislation, colonisation, public and even private morality and conduct. In the sphere of religion it doubtless

[1] Vide *Cults*, IV, pp. 161–162, 200–202.
[2] A fuller account will be found in *Cults*, IV, pp. 179–218.

emphasised the necessity of purification from blood-shed ; otherwise it had no high religious message to deliver ; but it was enthusiastic for the propagation of the cult of Dionysos, and it authorised and some-times encouraged the growing tendency towards the posthumous worship of distinguished men. In the sphere of morality its standard was generally high and its influence beneficent, especially—if we can trust the record—in the later period when it played the part of a State-Confessional and in its utterances reflected generally the progress of Greek ethics and the spirit of an enlightened humanitarianism.

But its chief religious achievements were to bring some principle of unity and authority into the com-plex and shifting aggregate of Greek polytheism, and to deepen the impression on the Hellenic mind of the divine ordering of the world ; and the fruits of this teaching we gather in the works of Attic tragedy and in the history of Herodotus.

In view of the history of other temple institutions of like power among other peoples—the Mesopo-tamian, for instance—we may be surprised that the Delphic priesthood made no attempt to impose Apollo as the supreme God upon the Hellenic states. The author of the Homeric hymn, composed partly under Delphic influences, exalts Apollo as high as he dares ; but neither in this nor in any Delphic utter-ance is Apollo presented as more than the minister of Zeus, the mouthpiece of the supreme Father-God, the tradition of whose supremacy among the Aryan Hellenes had been fixed fast by Homer and the Homeridai.

Nor did the Delphic Apollo succeed in achieving a monopoly of divination ; for the spirit of local independence was opposed to any divine monopoly in any department of life. And other oracles, such as some of those on the Asia Minor shore, acquired considerable prestige, especially in the later period when the influence of Delphi had declined. But from the eighth till the beginning of the fifth century, the Pythian is the only one of the many mantic institutions that is to be regarded as a vital force of Pan-Hellenism.

The games of Greece.—As another important phenomenon belonging to the earlier part of this second period we note the emergence and development of the great Hellenic games. Some recent theorists have supposed that all the public athletic contests in Greece arose directly from some religious ritual belonging to the cult either of the gods or of the dead hero. The evidence is faulty and the ritualistic origin of these institutions is unproven. But a common temple-worship undoubtedly gave the opportunity and the occasion to the development of the four Great Games, and from the beginning they were placed beneath the ægis of religion. And these must be reckoned as among the strongest Pan-Hellenic influences, evoking and strengthening the consciousness of nationality. For in the sixth century the whole of Hellas, eastern and western, was represented at Olympia, Pytho, the Isthmus and Nemea; here was maintained the 'truce of God' between the jealous or hostile communities; and at Olympia once in every four years the Pan-Hellenes offered a common homage to their aboriginal Father-God.

We must then regard the great games and the Pythian establishment as momentous factors in the religious national life, as tending to evolve a religion of a broader compass than the narrow tribal type of the remote past. And they concern the higher mental history of the race because most of them, and notably the Pythian, included competitions of art and literature ; and thus they assisted in establishing the specially Hellenic theory of the divine character of the artistic and intellectual life.

There were other festal and public meetings of a more exclusively religious purpose that also served to deepen in the various states the consciousness of spiritual unity, and often, where the great lyric poets composed hymns for the occasion, to exalt and illuminate the ideal conception of the divinity ; the Pan-Ionic Delian festival of Apollo, for instance, of which the splendour developed in the early post-Homeric age and with the growing prosperity of the new Ionic colonies, must have contributed much to the building up of the peculiarly Hellenic ideal of Apollo ; and the Homeric hymn, inspired by this occasion, is the earliest record of the national consciousness of the Ionic race.

Diffusion of Dionysos-worship.—Another religious phenomenon, pregnant of consequences for the spiritual history of Hellenism, is the diffusion of the worship of Dionysos. Faint, though indubitable traces of this can be discerned in the prehistoric period, but it only begins to be palpable and important in the early historic. Its significance has already been indicated in general outlines.[1]

Having entered Attica from Bœotia and been adopted into the Attic state-religion some time before the Ionic migration to the Asia Minor coast,

[1] Vide *supra*, pp. 34–35.

it gradually, in the eighth and seventh centuries captured most of the States of the Peloponnese, of the islands and the more distant colonies.

The Hellenic culture of Dionysos forms one of the most interesting chapters in the spiritual career of Hellenism ; for the taming of the wild Thracian God, the transformation of him into a civic deity, the disciplining and the adaptation of the thiasoi of the Maenads to the uses of an orderly state-religion, were not the least among the achievements of the Hellenic genius. And as the state-religion of these centuries had no eschatologic theory, so it seems to have discarded everywhere whatever eschatologic promise the Dionysiac religion proclaimed on its entrance into Greece. Yet, in spite of the chastening influence of the civic spirit, the worship preserved much of its distinctive tone and religious power ; evoking a special mood unknown in the other cults ; while even the savage form of sacrament, in which the God was devoured in his human or animal-incarnation, survived with some modifications in Tenedos and Chios down to a late period. The history, then, of the Dionysiac religion concerns the account of the development of the sacramental idea in the Mediterranean. It concerns also the history of Hellenic culture ; for one of its modes of expression was a peculiar type of emotional music, accompanying the Dionysiac hymn known as the dithyramb, which has been regarded, though probably erroneously, as the parent of Attic tragedy. Its main contribution to the polytheism of Greece was its stimulation of a warmer and stronger religious faith ; and its special later service to popular religious theory was the refining and

F

brightening of men's thoughts and sentiments concerning the life after death and the powers of the lower world, with whom the mild and genial God was generally identified or associated.

Orphic thiasoi.—But its highest importance is found rather in the esoteric than in the external or popular domain of Hellenic religion. For, perhaps as early as the seventh century, the cult of Dionysos was raised to a higher power by the rise and diffusion of the Orphic brotherhoods or 'thiasoi' who worshipped this deity under various mystic names. The study of Orphism is of the highest interest and complexity ; and it is only possible here to indicate its general features and significance. The preachers of the Orphic doctrines are the first propagandists or missionaries that we can discover in the pre-Christian Mediterranean world. For they had a definite message, and ignoring the gentile and civic barriers of the old political religion, they preached it, if not to all mankind, at least to all the Hellenes. It was a message fraught with some new and momentous ideas, whose real import we have been able to gather in part from the now famous gold-tablets found in the graves of Crete and South Italy, and containing parts of a metric Orphic liturgy and creed that is a product at latest of the fifth, if not the sixth, century B.C. Combining these with some passages in Pindar's Odes and Plato's Dialogues, we can recover in outline the doctrine of early Orphism. It proclaimed a theory, unfamiliar to native Greek mythology and religion, that the soul of man is divine and of divine origin ; that the body is its impure prison-house where it is in danger of contracting stain ; that by elaborate purifications and abstinences the soul might retain its purity, and by sacramental and magic methods the pure soul might enjoy in this life and in the next full communion with God. Preoccupied with the problem of the life after death, the Orphic mystics evolved the concept of Purgatory, a mode of posthumous punishment temporary and purificatory; also, if we can trust certain indications in Pindar and Plato, the dogma of reincarnation or more specially of a triple cycle of lives both in this world and the next. Students of religious philosophy have noted here the striking resemblance to Buddhistic thought; and have considered whether Indian speculation could have cast its influence so far westward at so early a time.

It is of more immediate importance for the religious history of the Greek people to determine— if we could—the measure of success that these missions achieved, how far they succeeded in capturing the masses or the élite of the people. They certainly did not succeed in penetrating the inner circle of the Eleusinian mysteries; there is no evidence that they even tried, though it is likely that they did; but we may surmise that their influence was at one time strong at Athens, as Aristophanes proclaims as a generally accepted tradition that Orpheus was the apostolic founder of all mysteries. They were evidently powerful in Crete; but the chief arena of their activity and the chief scene of their secular and political influence was 'Western Hellas' or Magna Græcia, where Pythagoras was their greatest convert and the Pythagorean clubs their militant orders. The career of these forms a page of general Greek history. Their downfall relieved Hellas from the danger of the establishment of Orphism as a secular power, which threatened the Hellenic spirit with a bondage to sacerdotalism and the pharisaic formalism of the purist. Henceforth, the Orphic religion was a private influence only, and we have no evidence to determine precisely how great it was at any particular epoch. Pindar was deeply touched by it. Æschylus and Sophocles, so far as we can see, remained unmoved, while Euripides may have been at times attracted and at times repelled but was in no sense its champion. Plato in a well-known passage[1] protests strongly against the Orphic mystery-mongers as spiritual quacks destitute of any real morality, who dealt in magic and traded in promises and threats concerning the other world. Whether this moral estimate of Orphism was just or not, there is no doubt that Plato's theory of the soul as expressed in the Phædrus was indebted to the Orphic metaphysic. And the part played by these preachers of purity and salvation in the later spiritual history of Greece was certainly of high importance. They mark the beginning of a new era of individualism and of what is called ' otherworldliness ' in religion ; for their concern was with the personal soul and its destiny.

Eleusinian mysteries.—The Eleusinia or Mysteries of Eleusis were a more national and Pan-Hellenic institution than the Orphica, but of somewhat similar influence and purpose. Originally they may have been merely the tribal mysteries of an agrarian society to which only the adult members of the Eleusinian community were admitted. But when our earliest record reveals them, namely, the Homeric hymn to Demeter which cannot be later

[1] *Republ.*, pp. 364–365.

than the close of the seventh century, they have already enlarged their borders and their scope. For they appear there as appealing to the whole Hellenic world, and their special promise to the initiated is the happiness of the soul after death. Having once transcended the tribal limits, they seem to have imposed no conditions on the aspirants for admission except the possession of Hellenic speech and purity from actual stain ; the initiation was open to women and occasionally to slaves. Nor does their influence and the power of their appeal appear to have waned until the introduction of Christianity. Many scholars have laboured to solve the problems concerning their ritual, their doctrine and their inner significance. It has been thought that their chief attractiveness may have lain in their preservation of a higher sacramental conception of the sacrifice that had died out in the ordinary public ritual ; that the initiate drank of a sacred cup in which were mystically infused the very life and substance of the kindly Earth-Mother, with whom their own being was thus transcendentally united. But more careful criticism shows that, though a simple form of sacrament was part of the preliminary service, the real pivot of the mystery was not this but a solemn pageant in which certain sacred things fraught with mystic power were shown to the eyes of the initiated, who also were allowed to witness mimetic performances showing the action and passion of a divine drama, the Abduction of the Daughter, the sorrow and long search of the Mother, the Holy Marriage of reconciliation, possibly the birth of a holy infant.

To imagine the thrill and the force of these rites, one must imagine a mediæval passion-play performed with surpassing stateliness and solemnity. Those who saw these things in the Hall of the Mysteries at Eleusis may have carried away with them an abiding sense of a closer communion with the benign powers of the nether world and a resulting hope of a happier posthumous lot. We must regard them as the highest and most spiritual product of the pure Hellenic religion, investing it with an atmosphere of mystery and awe that was generally lacking in the public cult, and which was unperturbed at Eleusis by any violence of morbid ecstasy such as marked the Phrygian and some of the Orphic rites. We may believe that they exercised a healthful influence on the moral and spiritual temperament of the Hellene ; but it is not clear that they definitely proclaimed any higher moral theory, nor do they appear like the Orphica to have preached any dogma of metaphysic or theology. But, like the Orphica, they tended to widen the horizon of the religious spirit ; for they appealed to a far larger public than the ordinary cults of the city ; and while being Pan-Hellenic in this sense they belong to the domain of personal religion, for they satisfied the personal craving of the individual for closer fellowship with the deity and they soothed the troublous apprehensions that were growing up in this second period concerning the individual destiny of the soul. Yet as regards Attica and Athens at least and probably as regards Hellas, they are not to be ranked, as the Orphica may be, among the disruptive forces of individualistic religion, undermining the social fabric of public worship. For the Athenian State administered them—by the help of Eleusinian officials—in its corporate capacity ; and one of the catechumens

—the παῖς ἀφ' ἑστίας—was initiated, according to the most probable view, in behalf of the whole youth of the city.[1]

In the great mysteries the agrarian significance, though discoverable and associated with simple agrarian magic, was overshadowed by higher and more spiritual religion. And elsewhere in the State-festivals we note this same phenomenon of progress in this second period. Old-world utilitarian rites of agriculture and fertility were often taken over by the expanding Polis and received an artistic elaboration that disguised their original significance for the primitive peasant and raised them to a higher plane of social religion. This interesting process can be best studied in following the detailed records of the Laconian Karneia and Hyakinthia, the Delphic Pythia, the Attic Panathenaia : we can feelingly appreciate in these the potent influence of the lyric poetry, the music, and the art of early Greece, shaping and elevating men's imagination of divinity.

By the close of this second period—c. 500 B.C.— the Hellenic national consciousness had realised itself in respect of intellectual culture, ethics and religion. Zeus Hellanios, the tribal God, is becoming Panhellanios. The age of the tyrants contributed much to the growth of Pan-Hellenism ; Peisistratos something to the idea of a national religion, in that he seems to have worked zealously for the organisation and expansion of the Eleusinian mysteries. The cult of Dionysos has penetrated the leading communities and most of the byways of Greece ; and nearly everywhere he has been partially tamed and the Mænads either suppressed or disciplined to the more sober purposes of civic worship.

[1] For more detailed discussion, vide Cults, 3, pp. 126–198.

But the two most striking phenomena in the spiritual history of the sixth century were, first, the rise and expansion of Ionic philosophy and physical specula-tion, and, secondly, the development of a new form of literature that came to be known as the Attic Drama. And both must be reckoned with among the forces affecting the life of the popular religion.

Sixth-century philosophy.—The relations of Greek philosophy to Greek religion is a great and complex subject, the theme of many modern treatises ; and in this slight sketch of the whole history of the polytheism there is no room for more than a few most general observations. So far as the new speculation, which gave birth to the free secular science of Europe, was preoccupied with questions of the physical origins of things and elemental theories of cosmogony, it would not necessarily clash with any orthodox prejudice of the average Hellene. For he had no sacred books which dictated to him any views concerning the origin of the world or the constitution of nature, and which he would have considered it immoral to disbelieve. In fact when Herakleitos boldly declared that "neither God nor man made the Kosmos," there was no authoritative Greek myth or theologic dogma to gainsay him. But the great philosophers of the sixth century, Pythagoras, Empedokles, Xeno-phanes and Herakleitos were also directly concerned with the philosophy of religion, with speculations on the nature and with the true definition of God-head ; and some of the surviving fragments of their works express ideas and sentiments in sharp antagonism to the concepts and ritual of the contemporary polytheism. The main trend of their speculations ran counter to the anthropomorphic theory of divinity ; and they tend to define God not as a person, but rather as the highest spiritual or metaphysical or even physical power or function of the universe ; and there is a common tendency in this sixth-century thought away from the theistic to the pantheistic view. Pythagoras is said to have explained the conception of God in terms of mathematics and to have been willing to accept the personages of the popular polytheism on condition of finding their true mathematical equation.[1] But this philosopher stands apart from the other leaders of this first period of Hellenic free thought. The mathematical mind is often a prey to mysticism. And Pythagoras was the most powerful champion and apostle of Orphism, the founder of those secret societies that threatened the secular and the intellectual freedom of Hellas. Equally on its mystic as on its rationalistic side the Pythagorean teaching was in tendency inimical to the public religion of Greece, though the members of this sect appear always to have compromised with it. In the fragments of Xenophanes we find the most severe protests against the current religious conceptions of Hellas ; his verses quoted by Clemens[2] polemise strongly against the folly of anthropomorphism, which is the master-passion of Greek polytheism ; and if one or two of his quoted utterances seem to proclaim monotheism, it is clear that for his higher thought Godhead was not a person, but a cosmic principle or a noetic idea. On the whole the same account may be given of the religious theory of Herakleitos so far as this is revealed at all in the

---

[1] Plut., *Mor.*, p. 881 E ; Porphyr., *Vit. Pyth.*, 19, 20.
[2] *Strom.*, V, p. 714.

fragments. It has indeed been recently maintained that he tolerated and found a place in his system for the contemporary polytheism ;[1] but it is probably a truer view that he regarded it with half-disguised contempt and only used its terms and figures on occasion as literary expressions ; while three of his fragments are scornful exclamations against the excesses of the Bacchic ritual, the methods of purification from blood, and the folly of idolatry.[2]

Yet in this early speculation of the sixth century the parting of the ways has not yet been reached for physical science and religion ; the cosmic theory is expressed in spiritual and animistic rather than in materialistic terms ; for Empedokles Love and Strife are creative principles, in the view of Thales the magnet has a soul and all things are full of divine potencies. The great movement of Ionic thought was indeed adaptable to a high pantheistic or animistic creed, but not to the personal polytheism of the Hellenes, though most of the philosophers do not appear to have been vehement protestants. And at first their protests could have influenced only the minds of a few ; not before the fifth century was the popular State-religion obliged to take notice of it.

Rise of tragedy.—The other phenomenon referred to above as marking the close of this period was the rise of tragedy. The question of its influence on the whole popular religion belongs to the history of the fifth century. What concerns us chiefly at this point is its close association with Dionysos-cult. The traditional view that it actually originated in some

---

[1] Vide Gilbert, " Speculation und Volksglaube in der Ionischen Philosophie," in *Arch. Relig. Wiss.*, 1910, p. 306.

[2] *Frag.*, CXXVI, CXXVII, CXXX (Bywater).

mimetic form of Bacchic ritual is in the opinion of the present writer still the most reasonable, although this is now denied by some scholars.[1] But even if its connection with Dionysos-worship is a secondary or accidental fact, it is still a fact of importance for the history of Greek polytheism. The records concerning Thespis of the Attic village Ikaria, a place dominated by ancient Dionysiac legend, the statement of Herodotus concerning Kleisthenes, the tyrant of Sikyon, who gave to Dionysos the tragic choruses that hitherto had been devoted to the hero-cult of Adrastos, are sufficient proofs that this greatest of all the literary achievements of post-Homeric Hellas was dedicated to the God already in the sixth century; and throughout the glorious career of the Attic stage Dionysos remained its patron-God.

His worship, then, must have received a strong stimulus from this new form of literature which rapidly achieved popularity and appealed directly to a larger public than the other. And his character thus undergoes a singular transformation; the wild God of barbaric origin comes to take rank by the side of Apollo and the Graces as a divinity of culture and education, the inspirer of one of the greatest of Hellenic arts. Here again, as in the cults of Apollo, Athena and the Muses, we mark the characteristically Hellenic fusion of art and religion; and the history of the dithyramb, the Dionysiac hymn which may have been the parent of the drama and which was wedded to a peculiar mode of music and rhythm, is an important chapter in the history of European music.

[1] Vide Ridgeway's *Origin of Tragedy*; his theory is criticised in *Hermathena*, 1912.

CHAPTER IV

THE THIRD PERIOD, 500–338 B.C.

THE third period of Greek religion may conveniently include the fifth century and that part of the fourth that ends with the downfall of the system of civic autonomy at the battle of Chaironeia. For the history of Greek religion as of Greek culture, it is of the highest interest, being the richest in respect of religious monuments and literature and the most forceful and momentous in regard to the influences at work. In the sphere of external history it witnessed such world-crises as the struggle of Hellenism against barbarism, the rise and fall of the Imperial City-State, and the emergence of Macedon as a world-power; in the sphere of culture it witnessed the culmination of the greatest art of the world, the bloom and maturity of the Attic drama and Pindar's lyric, the diffusion of education and the spirit of enquiry through the activity of the Sophists, and the higher development of philosophy and science. To show how the religious practice and theory of the higher and lower members of Hellenic society were affected by the great events and achievements of this greatest period of human history is a necessary but a difficult task.

Fifth-century religion contrasted with the Homeric. —If we take Athens as the typical religious community of the fifth century and compare the

structure and forms of her state-polytheism with
those of the old Homeric world, we find the personalities of the prehistoric pantheon still worshipped
and cherished ; no prehistoric cult of that epic
world has as yet fallen into desuetude ; nor had the
most civilised city of Hellas discarded the immemorial rites of the simple peasant religion, the
worship of rivers and streams, nor some of the most
naïve practices of animism. And it is clear that this
conservatism was no hieratic convention, but a
living faith, expressing a religious intuition of the
people, who were as yet untouched by the cooling
influences of science and philosophic scepticism. In
fact, for the greater part of the fifth century, the life
of the polytheism was probably stronger than it had
been ever in the past. It was strengthened by the
admission of a few new figures and by the development of some of the old.[1]

It is rather in respect to its spirit, tone and outlook that the religion of the fifth century presents
some striking contrasts to the Homeric. Its
anthropomorphism is even more pronounced, thanks
to its great art-power, but it reveals a deeper
conviction concerning the part played by moral
agencies and powers in the affairs of men. The
writings of Herodotus expound a religious view of
history of which only faint indications were found
in the earlier epic literature. The historian of the
fifth century regards the momentous contest of
Greece with Persia as a conflict of moral forces, the
issue being worked out by unseen powers, such as
Nemesis, Violence and Justice, with Zeus as the

[1] Pan, the daimon-god of flocks, came in from Arcadia at the
beginning of this century (vide *Cults*, V, p. 431) ; Asklepios, with
his circle from Epidauros, at the close.

righteous Judge. And in weaving into his narrative the stories of Æacid heroes and the Eleusinian deities speeding to the help of the Hellenes at Salamis, he doubtless represents the faith of the average Greek. A similar view was also impressed on the religious imagination of the people by oracular utterances, such as that which was imputed to the prophet Bakis—Δῖα Δίκη σβέσσει κρατερὸν Κόρον, Ὕβριος υἱόν,[1] "Justice divine shall quench fell Koros, the child of Insolence," Koros standing for Persia, the tyranny born of satiety. It is expressed pictorially on the famous vase at Naples, representing Hellas and Asia pleading their cause before the High God with Ἀπάτη, as a tempting demon, standing by Asia.[2] In this scene we trace also the influence of the famous tragedy of Æschylus, the 'Persæ,' which in more than one passage of deep religious conviction pronounces moral judgment on the great event.[3] The same view is expressed and the same tone heard in the striking poem of Pindar's eighth Pythian ode, where he exults over the triumph of 'Hesychia,' the armed Peace of Hellas, who has cast Insolence into the sea, even as Zeus quelled the monster Typhœus.

Pan-Hellenism.—The Hellenic confederate effort against Persia was the nearest approach ever made by the Hellenic race to Pan-Hellenic action; and in a striking chapter of Herodotus, eulogising the loyalty of the Athenians to the cause of Greece, emphasis is laid on the name of Zeus Hellenios.[4] This is the highest political title of the High God;

---

[1] Herod., 8, 77.
[2] Heydemann, *Die Vasensammlungen des Museum Nazionale zu Neapel*, 3253.
[3] Vide specially 1. 805–808, 822–824.   [4] 9, 7, 4.

and its history is interesting. Originally the narrow tribal name of the God of the Hellenes, a small Thessalian group under the leadership of the Aiakidai, it was transported to Aigina by a migration of the same tribe, whose ancestor Aiakos was the high-priest of Zeus Hellanios ; already in the sixth century, when the denotation of Hellas was enlarged, the title may have taken on a wider meaning. But it was the danger of the Persian wars, and the part played in them—we may believe—by the men and the old heroes of Aigina that brought the cult into prominence, investing the cult-name with a wider significance and a more potent appeal. Here, then, was Hellenic religion giving voice to an ideal that might be realised by the poet, the artist, and the thinker, but never by any statesman or state.

Another cult belonging to the same range as this was that of Zeus Eleutherios, the God of Hellenic freedom. "Having driven out the Persian they raised an altar to Zeus, the God of the free, a fair monument of freedom for Hellas."[1] These lines of Simonides commemorate the dedication of the Greeks after the victory at Platæa, when they had purified the land and its shrines from the polluting presence of the barbarian by means of sacred fire brought from Delphi. The significance of this has been pointed out elsewhere[2] by the present writer ; the fight for liberty was prompted by more than a mere secular passion, but by an idea inherent in the civic religion. The title Ελευθέριος is only known before the Persian wars in the Zeus-worship of Laconia ; henceforth it was widely diffused, commemorating not only the deliverance of Greece from

---

[1] Bergk, *Frag.*, 140.   [2] *Hibbert Lectures*, 83–84.

the barbarian, but, in Sicily for instance, emancipation from the domestic tyrant.

In contrast with the deterioration of the old Roman religion, caused by the Hannibalic wars, the successful struggle of Greece against barbarism in the east and the west undoubtedly quickened for a time the fervour and devotion inspired by the national cults. The sufferings of Hellas were easily repaired ; the Gods in whom they had trusted had not failed them, and much of the spoils won from the barbarian were gratefully dedicated to the embellishment of the shrines. The vacillating and time-serving policy of Delphi at the hour of the greatest peril was condoned or unnoted by the victors, and Apollo received an ample share of the fruits of victory. The champions of Hellenism in the West, Gelo and Hiero, commemorated their victories over the Carthaginian and Etruscan powers at Himera and Kyme by thankofferings sent to Apollo at Delphi and Zeus at Olympia. The bronze helmet found at Olympia, and now in the British Museum, inscribed with the simple dedication, " Hieron the son of Deinomenes and the Syracusans send Tuscan spoils to Zeus from Kyme," is an epoch-marking monument of Pan-Hellenic history and religion. The gratitude of Hellas was paid in the first instance to the High God Zeus ; to him was consecrated the ' feast of freedom ' at Platæa, which was still commemorated with pathetic fervour even in the last days of Hellenic decay ;[1] to him, under the national title of Olympios, was dedicated the mighty temple at Akragas, from the spoils won by Gelo at Himera. But the outflow of national

---

[1] Plut., *Vit. Arist.*, 20 ; Paus., 9, 2, 5.

thankfulness was directed to other divinities as well ; notably and naturally to the War-Goddess of the Athenians, and the spoils of Persia at Athens and Platæa were partly devoted to the erection of two striking statues of Athena. Nor were the lesser powers of the elements forgotten ; the winds that assisted the Greek fleet at Artemision and the nymphs of the soil on which the battle of Platæa was fought ; the grateful Athenians instituted a cult of Boreas, their kinsman, in their restored city and assisted in the worship of the Nymphs at Kithairon. The Arcadian goatherd-God, the rustic Pan, was admitted into Athens shortly before the battle of Marathon, and the story to which the Athenians gave currency of the help he rendered them at the great battle contributed something no doubt to the subsequent diffusion of his cult.

A further religious consequence of these great events was the stimulus given to hero-worship ; Gelo, the victor at Himera, and some of the Hellenes who fell at Thermopylæ, Marathon and Platæa received heroic honours. This ' heroising ' of the recently defunct had its moral value as a strong stimulus to patriotism, when they had died in the service of their country ; and though it was degraded in the fifth century to the exaltation of the useless athlete, yet it must be reckoned among the life-forces of later polytheism and as a momentous factor of higher religious history.

Finally, we may with probability ascribe to the triumph of Hellas and to the expanding glory and greatness of Athens a marked increase in the Hellenic popularity of the Eleusinian mysteries. For this the Athenians might thank Herodotus and his thrilling narrative of the vision of a heavenly host seen moving from Eleusis towards Salamis, for the salvation of Hellas ; they might also thank their own far-sighted policy of encouraging the whole Hellenic world to take part in the worship at Eleusis, aspiring thus to make the Hall of the Mysteries, a recent architectural work of the Periclean administration, the centre of a Pan-Hellenic faith.[1] And their attempt in great measure succeeded.

Influence of religious art.—The study of the polytheism of this century is essentially also a study of the great religious art which culminated in the handiwork of Pheidias, but which continued forceful and prolific till the age of Alexander. The general effect of the iconic art upon Greek religion has been briefly indicated above ; and long before this century the religious bias of the race was committed to idolatry ;[2] the people craved an image that they could love and cherish, though here and there they might retain the uncouth fetich, the block of wood or rudely hewn stone, because of the immemorial magic which it had acquired through ages of shy half-savage veneration. The achievement of Pheidias and his contemporaries was only the culmination in a process of ideal anthropomorphism that began with Homer and was helped forward by the lyric poetry and music of the post-Homeric age and by the art of the sixth century. Strictly estimated and studied in all its fullness, in the marvellous products of vase-painting, glyptic and sculpture that even the shattered fabric of antiquity presents to us, the art of the fifth and early fourth century must be called the most perfect religious art

[1] Vide *Cults*, III, pp. 156–157.   [2] Vide *supra*, pp. 36–37.

of the world. A more spiritual or more mystic religion could not have produced or could not have borne with such an art. But it was the best and most satisfying expression of the best that the religious spirit of Hellenism admitted ; for this polytheism had been built up by the teachers of the people, poets and artists obeying the race-instinct, not on vague conceptions of infinite Godhead ineffable for art and inexpressible in clear speech, but on vivid perceptions of concrete divine person-ages, distinct in form, attributes and character robust and very real. The Greek artist, with his miraculous cunning of hand, could deal with such types as he could not have dealt with ' the Word ' or with the ' Buddha.' Nor was he merely the exponent of the highest popular imagination, but, unconsciously perhaps and in obedience to a true art-tradition, at times a reformer and in any case a creator. For us his works have this value among others that, even more than the poetic literature, they reveal to us how the people at their best imagined their deities. But they also helped the people to imagine them better and more nobly. Perhaps the earliest art of Hellas that takes rank among the works of high religious inspiration are the Attic vase-paintings produced near to 500 B.C. that portray the thiasos of Dionysos. The strong spirit of that religion that lifted the votary above the conventional moral human life, the wild joy of self-abandonment, the ecstasy of communion with the God, all are here more startlingly expressed than even in the lyrics of the Bacchæ of Euripides or in the single perfect Bacchic ode of Sophocles' Anti-gone. It was not till the time of Skopas in the fourth

century that Greek sculpture could so deal with this
orgiastic theme. The plastic work of the fifth
century dealing with divine forms is mainly tranquil, majestic, ethical, intellectual ; the physical
perfection of the divinities sculptured on the
Parthenon impresses us not merely and not so much
with the sense of physical beauty and strength, but
rather with the sense of a higher and nobler vital
power ; so instinct is the beauty with that quality
that the Greeks called σεμνότης, a quality partly
ethical, partly spiritual, but palpable in material
forms that hint at a tranquil reserve of strength.
The expressive power of such an art can show
benignity and mildness of mood without senti-
mentality, because without voluptuousness, intellectual thought without morbidness, majesty without self-display.

The gentle and tranquillising spirit of the
Eleusinian mysteries speaks in the famous Eleusinian
relief showing the mother and the maid giving his
mission to Triptolemos. The Pheidian Athena
Parthenos was a more deeply conceived ideal than
the Athena of the poets, for it showed her as the
Madonna of the Athenian people, with a softer
touch of maternal gentleness in the face. The Zeus
Olympios of Pheidias transcended the portrait of the
High God as given by Homer or even by Æschylus ;
for the chryselephantine statue impressed the later
Greeks as the ideal of the benign and friendly deity,
the divine patron of a Hellas united and at peace
with itself ; an image that appeared " to add something to the traditional religion,"[1] embodying, as
Dio Chrysostom says, a conception of the God so

[1] Quintil., *Inst. Orat.*, 12, 10, 9.

convincing and complete that " having once seen it one could not imagine him otherwise."[1]

Nor had any of the poets presented Hera in forms so winning and gracious as those in which the best art of this age embodied her, as the Argive Goddess ' of good works ' " in whose face and person brightness appeared by the side of majesty."[2] The poetic presentation of Apollo is blurred and incomplete compared with such plastic types as the Apollo of the Parthenon frieze and the Pheidian statue in the Museo delle Terme. The older poetic ideal of Aphrodite was shallow and trite compared to the Aphrodite of the Pheidian type, such as we see presented by the Laborde head in the Louvre ; here is something of the majesty of the great cosmic goddess imagined by Æschylus in his Danaides, but combined with an emotion of human love in the countenance and a winning appeal that the verses of the great poet do not clearly convey. And we may surmise that the ' Ourania ' Aphrodite of Pheidias had some influence on the theory of Plato and his distinction between the heavenly and the sensual love. The full imagination of the personality of Kore would combine the radiance and the grace of the young cornfield with the awe and mystery of the lower world ; the former is masterfully presented by a coin[3] of Lampsakos that shows her rising from among the cornstalks with uplifted yearning face ; the unknown artist of the great Syracusan medallion struck towards the close of the fifth century combines this aspect of her, in a type of surpassing

---

[1] *Or.*, 53, p. 401.   [2] Vide *Cults*, 1, p. 231.
[3] *Cults*, Vol. III, Coin Pl. No. 2 ; Gardner's *Types of Greek Coins*, Pl. 10, 25.

loveliness, with a touch of melancholy that hints at the character of the Goddess of death.[1]

And yet this triumphant anthropomorphic art must have failed, and judged by the fragments that survive did fail, when it tried to reveal in clear outline and full light the half-shrouded forms of the nether world, the Chthonian Goddesses and the Eumenides whose nature appealed to the sense of religious awe, to what the Greeks called τὸ φρικῶδες, and did not brook to be wholly revealed. We may doubt therefore if even the statues of the Holy Ones, the Semnai, carved by Kalamis and Skopas, were types so expressive of the real moral-religious imagination that fashioned these figures of cult as were certain awestruck verses of Sophocles in the Œdipus Coloneus. Nevertheless, this ideal Greek art, by expressing in palpable forms of benign beauty the half-palpable personages of the lower world, did one service to religion and the religious imagination ; it banished the uncouth and the terrible and helped to purge and tranquillise the Greek mind by investing the Chthonian powers with benevolence and grace. We discern here the influence of the Bacchic and Demeter mysteries working upon the artist and of the artist upon the popular faith. That the average Greek of the classic period was saved from the vampire terrors that Mr. Lawson has discovered in modern Greece[2] was due equally to the religion and to the art that he saw around him.

Apart from this special fact, a phenomenon so momentous in the spiritual world as the flowering of this religious art in the fifth century claims

---

[1] Vide *Cults*, III, pp. 271–272, Coin Pl. No. 18.
[2] *Modern Greek Folklore and Ancient Greek Religion.*

prominent notice even in the slightest sketch of the whole history of Greek religion ; for it must have worked an effect which no student of insight would be tempted to belittle upon the religious mood and thought of the people. Greek records sufficiently attest its religious working ; even the alien Roman, Æmilius Paulus, when he approached the Pheidian masterpiece of Zeus Olympios felt the thrill of the ' real presence '[1] ; when Aristophanes fervently calls on Athena as " the Maiden who holdeth our city in her hand and alone hath visible power and might and is called the Warder of the Gate,"[2] he is thinking of the bronze statue carved by Pheidias and set to guard the entrance to the Akropolis.

It is impossible, then, that this beautiful idolatry, against which the philosophers might occasionally protest,[3] could have weakened the popular faith in the native deities. Introduced suddenly into Rome it helped to destroy the old Roman animistic religion. But the religious instinct and history of Greece was wholly different from that of Rome. Greek polytheism would probably have perished or been transformed by alien systems of cult far sooner than it was, if Greek art had not fortified and ennobled it, rooting it deeply in the æsthetic-religious emotions and perceptions of the people. By establishing so convincingly the individuality of the Greek divinities, it preserved them from a too rapid absorption into the personalities of Oriental religions, when the fusion of west and east had been achieved by Alexander and his successors.

---

[1] Livy, 45, 28.   [2] *Thesmoph.*, 1136.

[3] Xenophanes' protest in the sixth century is the most noticeable, Clem., *Strom.*, 5, pp. 714–715 P. The Stoic theory of Zeno condemned the erection of temples as well as idols, *ib.*, p. 691 P.

Influence of Literature : Pindar, Æschylus, Sophocles.—More familiar and apparently more answerable is the question concerning the influence of the poetic masterpieces of this period, the works of Pindar and the Attic drama, on the general history of Greek religion. The subject is obviously too complex for the scope of this summary, and has been handled by many scholars in large treatises. There is only room here for the most general statement of facts, tendencies and effects. As exponents of the highest contemporary religious thought the names of Pindar, Æschylus, Sophocles and Euripides are those of primary authority. It is easy and interesting to collect religious citations from their works, to compare these one with another and with the current polytheism. It is far more difficult to decide generally and in regard to any special point how far any one of them could have influenced or modified the popular religion. Nor are all these four on the same footing in respect of opportunity. For Pindar writes for dynasts and aristocrats and, being a hireling, might be thought fettered in the free expression of his sentiments ; and in any case his public was more limited than that which the three dramatists addressed. Therefore their message was likely to reach further and to penetrate the Greek mind more deeply than anything that Pindar had to say ; and that this was actually the case can be proved. Nevertheless, Pindar must be reckoned with as an original thinker who spoke words of power ; in spite of his profession, his mind remained imperial and free ; and in his attitude to the public religion he is to be grouped with Æschylus and Sophocles ; and all three stand together and apart from Euripides. All three show the virility, the mental tranquillity combined with imagination and audacity, that marked the typical character of the greatest age of Hellas. And all three genially and without querulous protest, though with some freedom of criticism, accept the existing religious order, desiring to ennoble it, not to destroy it. Pindar himself was the establisher of certain new cults, and the first great literary preacher in Greece of Orphic eschatology, and, we may say, the first great poet in Europe who raised the theme of Paradise to the level of the highest poetry. Such a marvel of song on the mysteries of life and death as the second Olympian ode was a new voice in Hellas ; how far it echoed, and with what influence on the faith of the people, is impossible to measure with accuracy. For the progress of this new eschatology, which is a weighty subject for the history of later Hellenism, we have some important negative evidence in the fact that neither Æschylus nor Sophocles show any knowledge of Orphism or interest in it, or any preoccupying concern with the state of the soul after death ; nor in their occasional utterances concerning posthumous judgment do they go beyond the popular traditional view : though the thoughtful refinement of Sophocles suggested to him that there might be forgiveness of sins and reconciliation after death.[1] Nor do we find anywhere in the works of the two dramatists any hint of that pregnant Orphic doctrine to which Pindar gives voice, that humanity is of divine origin—ἐν ἀνδρῶν ἐν Θεῶν γένος—a doctrine which passed into the higher thought of later Greece.

[1] *Antig.*, 521.

Leaving aside this special question, we find a certain general resemblance in the religious view of these earlier poets of the fifth century. All three preach the supremacy of Zeus, his omnipotence and perfect justice, while Sophocles lays stress on his mercy. The effect of this poetic message was probably great and certainly timely ; for the growing power and frequency of hero-cult, which Pindar himself and the dramatists indirectly encouraged, was a danger to the higher religion ; and the backward and less cultured Hellenes were doubtless liable to the propensity of the savage mind to prefer the worship of the local daimon to that of the high God. Against such degeneracy the works of the greatest fifth-century poets, like the masterpiece of the greatest fifth-century sculptor, served at least as an enduring protest in Hellas.

And it would be of interest to consider how far the sculptor, in regard to the general conception of his mighty theme and in the choice of mystic bywork whereby he made it articulate, drew certain suggestions from the poetry of Æschylus.

These poets also deal with the question of Fate and Destiny. The personal, or half-personal, Μοῖρα was an old but insignificant figure of the popular religion and mythology, and Homer is aware of her and has to reckon with her. She might become more formidable under the philosophic conception of τὸ εἱμαρμένον which appeared in the philosophy of Herakleitos ; and we know that later philosophy and cultivated thought was much perplexed over the problem of the reconciliation of Fate with the idea of a free divine Providence. The great Attic poets, taking their cue from Homer, "follow a short cut," interpreting Moira as the voice or agent or emanation of the power of Zeus.[1] And the pupil of Pheidias, Theokosmos of Megara, was working out the same idea when he carved the Fates with the Hours as subordinate adjuncts to the great form of Zeus.[1] We may say, then, that both the poetry and the art of this period worked for the deliverance of the polytheism from the burden of fatalism, which tends to lower the value and sap the force of all personal religion.

The Prometheus Vinctus of Æschylus expresses indeed a view of Zeus that conflicts with the higher religious thought of the poet. But Æschylus has here taken up a crude story that he cannot wholly moralise. On the other hand, his handling of the idea of the curse in the house of Pelops is not worked out on the lines of mechanical fatalism ; one is made to feel it as a spiritual atmosphere which engenders a bias towards evil, but does not overpower the freedom of the individual.

Again, each of these poets, while accepting and in certain points purifying the traditional polytheism, was capable of religious thought that worked on other lines than anthropomorphism. The High God, Zeus, is generally for them a definite personal Being ; but once at least Æschylus transcends this apprehension of him and defines Zeus pantheistically as a supreme cosmic force ; a fragment of his 'Heliades' speaks of him thus : " Zeus is air, earth, heaven ; Zeus is the whole of things, and whatsoever is higher still than these." Moreover, the other divine forces that shape our lives are presented by him and his fellow-poets, not always as θεοί, but as moral

[1] Paus., 1, 40, 4.

powers that are only half-personal, not as concrete individual deities, but as emanations of the divinity. We may call them ' personifications of moral ideas,' and some are no more than what this phrase implies, such as those for instance with which Euripides capriciously plays. But some may be rather described as the Soul-powers of the High God, like, in some ways, to the Persian Fravashi ; such are Pindar's Σώτειρα Διὸς Ξενίου Θέμις,[1] the Dike of Æschylus, " Justice, the Maiden Daughter of God,"[2] who "shines in the poor man's smoke-dimmed cabin " ;[3] Mercy in the verse of Sophocles,[4] " Mercy shares the throne of God to deal with all the deeds of men." While Pindar's genius inclines to the brighter of these emanations, Æschylus broods rather over the gloomy forces of the shadowy world, which he might at times be constrained to present in palpable concrete form for stage purposes and yet his own deeper thought could grasp as half-outlined spiritual powers, not the less real because im- palpable. The ordinary Hellene in his religious perceptions laid too much stress on personal indi- viduality, as if this were the only criterion of ideal reality ; from his point of view if Eros was to be a real power of the divine world, then Eros must be imagined as a beautiful youth. But Kypris or Aphrodite in a striking Sophoclean fragment is no longer presented as a personal goddess, but as a diffused pantheistic force.[5] And the Attic drama may have enlarged the mental outlook of the suc- ceeding generations in this matter ; for the author of the speech against Aristogeiton in the fourth

---

[1] *Ol.*, 8, 28.   [2] *Sept. c. Theb.*, 662.   [3] *Agam.*, 776.
[4] *Oed. Col.*, 1268.   [5] *Trag. Græc. Frag.* (Nanck), 855.

century must have been sure that his audience would understand him when he said, " all mankind have altars dedicated to Justice, Law-abidingness and Pity, the fairest and holiest (being those) in the very soul and the nature of each individual."[1] This is just how Euripides might speak.

The great fifth-century poets were all moralists each in his own way. The history of Greek ethics only concerns us at the several points where it touches religion ; and to this history, both generally and on its religious side, the works of Pindar and the three dramatists make important contributions. Of special interest is their attitude to Greek mythology which, in spite of its general brightness and beauty, seriously needed in parts the puritanical reformer, if it was to be harmonised with the higher religious thought. But none of these poets, not even the grave Æschylus, was willing to undertake such a rôle. Pindar of all the three comes nearest to preaching, for his *métier* allowed him more personal freedom of comment. While following, on the whole, the beaten path of tradition, he could innovate or invent if a moral purpose was to be gained ; for instance, he preaches to a friend the doctrine of forgiveness of injuries and confirms it by the example of Zeus, who forgave and released the Titans, a myth for which he is the sole authority.[2] We find him anticipating Plato in his protest against some grotesque and repulsive stories, such as the cannibalism of the Gods in the myth of Pelops, or blasphemous stories, such as the theomachies and the combats of heroes against divinities : " let all war and strife stand far apart from the immortals "[3]

[1] § 35.   [2] *Pyth.*, 4, 517.   [3] *Ol.*, 9, 60.

is a good sententious maxim for the expurgation of
Greek mythology and for the enrichment of Greek
ethico-religious thought.   But neither Pindar nor
the two older dramatists protest against the more
licentious myths, and they accept at need various
legends about the amours of the Gods.   In fact, the
axiom that sexual purity was an essential attribute
of all divinity was not yet accepted by the higher
thought of Greece.

Pindar's freedom and sense of irresponsibility in
regard to myths has a certain value in that it shows
that the futilities and improprieties of mythology—
the " unhappy stories of bards "—were not necessarily a burden on the stronger religious minds of
Hellas, and that they could be greatly excised from
the polytheism without endangering the popular
worship and faith, which in the main was independent of them.

As for the two dramatists, his contemporaries,
mythology was their public business, and they
accepted it genially because they were not, in the
first place, moral teachers, but dramatists ; it did
not therefore occur to them to protest or violently
to reform.   But they might select, discard and
reshape ; they could take the great legends of the
past, legends of Thebes, the story of the Niobids, of
Prometheus, the death of Ajax, all of them irrecon-
cilable in parts with higher morality and religion,
and invest them with as much morality as the
tradition admitted.   This they did with force and
subtlety.   And generally the moral spirit and
imagination of Æschylus and Sophocles must be
counted among the spiritual facts of this period with
which the history of Greek ethics and religion must

deal. Doubtless the older and robuster poet was the stronger moral and religious force ; his protests against the non-moral doctrine of Nemesis, his profound utterances concerning moral responsibility and the moral continuity that links our lives and actions, his discovery that suffering brings moral wisdom—these are landmarks in the ethical story of Greece ; while with Sophocles the conviction is no less deep of the eternity and divinity of the moral law.

They were the last spokesmen of a civic-imperial system with a civic religion and morality that had not yet passed its zenith.

Euripides.—The part played by Euripides in this spiritual history of Hellas was wholly different. Younger contemporary of Sophocles as he was, he seems to belong to a different age. In his work and thought is reflected far more vividly than in the older poets of the same century the new mental life which was fostered by the philosophers and the sophists. The influence of the physical speculations of the sixth century and of those of Demokritos and Anaxagoras of the fifth, which at some points advanced further in materialism, has had time to penetrate the more gifted minds and to compel the public to a certain attention. The paid ' Sophist,' the pioneer of modern education and the first champion of the critical spirit, was travelling around. And after 470 B.C. the imperial greatness of Athens had begun to attract the greatest teachers and thinkers of the age. It was of great moment for Euripides that such men as Anaxagoras and Prota-goras were active in Athens for many years, and that he had enjoyed familiar intercourse with them as he also enjoyed with Sokrates. It is clear that the poet imbibed deeply their teaching and their spirit ; he was also learned in Orphism, antiquarianism and remote folklore. Being by nature a great poet, he has also something of the weakness of the ' polymath ' or the ' intellectual ' ; he had not the steadiness of brain or strong conviction enough to evolve a systematic philosophy or clear religious faith ; his was, in fact, the stimulating, eager, critical spirit, not the constructive. His mental sympathies and interests shift and range from pole to pole. He is a secularist in his view of a physical universe, and he foreshadows a secular treatment of ethics based on ideas of $\phi \acute{v} \sigma \iota s$ and heredity, though a chorus of his maidens may praise chastity as " the fairest gift of the Gods." It was therefore possible, though most unjust, that Aristophanes should call him an atheist. On the other hand, he is capable of profound religious sentiment and exalted religious utterance, and strikes out flashes of light that might kindle and illuminate a higher religion. Therefore it was possible for Clemens of Alexandria to find in some of his words a foreshadowing of Christ.[1] He remains for us an enigma, and probably no final judgment will ever be pronounced upon him, in which we shall all agree.

But the student of Greek religion must confront these two questions about him : (*a*) What was his real sentiment concerning the popular religion ? (*b*) What were his contributions to religious thought, and what was likely to be his influence on the religious temperament ? To make up one's mind on these questions demands a long and critical study,

---

[1] *Strom.*, p. 688.

also a tactful sense of the distinction between Euripides the playwright and Euripides the thinker. It is the confusion of this distinction that leads, for instance, to the strangely erroneous views held concerning the religious significance of his ' Bacchæ.' A sympathetic reading of many of the plays must convey the impression that certain cult-figures and legends of the polytheism filled the poet with scorn and loathing ; and at times he seems to compose as if he had a personal hatred of Apollo and Aphrodite in particular, for instance, in the Ion and Hippolytus. When he can interpret Aphrodite as a cosmic force he can dilate on this as beautifully and ardently as Lucretius ; if he could have believed that Apollo was merely the Sun, as he tells us ' the wise ' were well aware, he might have forgiven him. But it is the real personal Aphrodite of Homer and Helen, the personal Apollo, the father of Ion, the seducer of Kreusa, and the beloved ancestor of the Athenians, that rankled in his mind. When he handles the story of the madness of Herakles and brings madness on the stage, he uses her first as his mouthpiece to convey to the Athenians what he thought of Hera ;[1] just as he puts into the mouth of Amphitryon his own mordant criticism of the action of Zeus.[2] Yet with other parts of the polytheism he seems at times in the most glowing sympathy ; in the Hippolytus, for instance, where he expresses for the first time in literature the religious rapture of purity ; in the Bacchæ where he discovers the necessary phrase for the expression of the Bacchic communion, for the ecstasy of the Mænad-revel on the mountain, in verses that tingle with the nature-

---

[1] *Herc. Fur.*, 1. 847–858.   [2] *Ib.*, 339–347.

H

magic which was at the root of this wild cult. Yet
no one should be deceived into thinking that he is
preaching the cause of Dionysiac worship ; for the
Bacchæ closes with that depressing anti-climax,
where Dionysos plays the sorriest part, and Euripides' own sour dislike of the personal traditional
God gives an unpleasant flavour to the last scene.
It is this bitterness of protestantism and criticism in
this poet that strikes a new note in Greece ; and
Euripides may be regarded as the first in European
history to be possessed with the theologic temper.
It cannot be said that he preached a new religion ;
he was no votary even of Orphism, for though, as the
Bacchæ and the fragment of his ' Cretans ' attest, he
felt something of its spell, he was not of that cast of
mind that could be deceived by its pharisaic ritual
and laws of diet, and he certainly cherished no
mystic belief concerning the life after death ; for
even in the ' Bacchæ ' there is no reference to this
attractive dogma, which was the main anchor of the
Orphic faith. Nor can he be truly described as a
zealous reformer of the people's faith and practice ;
for the reformer must have some belief in that which
he wishes to reform ; and that Euripides firmly
believed in any part of the polytheism is hard to
maintain ; his final attitude is generally a doubt.
Nevertheless, his protests might have been of value
to the more cultured citizen who still clave to his
civic worship. They are directed mainly and most
forcibly against the stories of divine vindictiveness
and divine licentiousness. He is evidently touched
with the new idea that vengeance is alien to the
perfect nature of God ; this was still more insistently
proclaimed by Plato and by the Pythagoreans and

later philosophers.[1]   On the second count his protest is suggested by the notion that was dawning in him that purity in every sense was essential to the divine nature ; he is then the herald in literature of a thought which Orphism may have prompted and which was to play a leading part in later religion and religious speculation, but which was unfamiliar to his contemporaries either in Hellas or anywhere in the Mediterranean except in Israel.   His leading principle of criticism in all these matters is expressed in the Iphigeneia in Tauris, namely, that the evil in religious practice and legend arises from men imputing their own evil nature to God.[2]   We owe much to the man who first uttered this warning against a debasing anthropomorphism.

The immoral elements in Greek mythology, which have been constantly reprobated by ancient and modern writers, have often blinded them to the fact that Greek religion in its forms of worship and sacred formulæ was mainly pure and refined.   The stories about the Gods, often of the type natural to savage folklore, did not constitute ancient religion ; and they were the less able to choke the growth of a higher ethical-religious spirit in that they were not enshrined in sacred books that could speak with authority to the people.   Yet we have not infrequent proofs in Greek literature, notably in Plato's *Euthyphron*, that they might exercise at times an immoral influence on men's conduct.   Meantime the educational movement in the sixth and fifth centuries had awakened men's minds to the importance of the moral question in literature.   And the protests of Euripides are developed by Plato in his

---

[1] Vide my *Hibbert Lectures*, p. 114.   [2] l. 391.

scheme of education in the *Republic*, and the same point of view prompts him to his puritanical legislation against poets. Such moral movements in the polytheistic societies of Greece are interesting to mark, though their effect is often difficult to estimate. The new puritanical spirit had probably a wholesome influence on the more cultured minds ; it had little influence on the mass of the people, nor does the later poetry of the Hellenistic period show much trace of it.

As regards the actual forms of Greek ritual and worship, Euripides has nothing revolutionary to say. He appears to have a strong dislike for prophets, and in this he was in some accord with Æschylus, Sophocles, and the Athenian people. He shows great distrust for Delphi ; and its influence was doubtless impaired at Athens during the Peloponnesian war. He protests against human sacrifice as a barbaric and non-Hellenic institution[1]—though he appears fond of it as a dramatic motive—and on one occasion the speaker argues that the Gods need nothing from mortals at all ;[2] the thought was suggested merely by dramatic exigencies ; and Euripides nowhere attempts a crusade against the value of sacrifice in general. He has only one important thing to say about it, namely that the small sacrifice of the pious often outweighs the hecatomb.[3] This thought implies a more spiritual view of the divine nature and is not infrequently expressed in the later literature ; according to Theophrastos and Theopompos this higher view of sacrifice was even encouraged by the Delphic oracle.[4]

---

[1] *Iphig Taur.*, 1. 391.   [2] Clem., *Strom.*, p. 691 P.
[3] Vide Stobæ, *Flor.*, Vol. IV (Meineke), p. 264.
[4] Vide *Cults*, Vol. IV, p. 210.

There is much indeed in the sententious poetry of Euripides that might have elevated and cleared the religious thoughts of his age ; but it is doubtful if his ultimate conception of Godhead, as it tends towards pantheism, could have been reconciled with the anthropomorphic polytheism of the people or if those most conversant with his tone and inspired by his spirit could have remained long in sympathy with orthodoxy. And there is an instinct in Euripides which enhances his value for the modern man, but which was to be subversive in the longrun of the old civic religion, namely, the humanitarian or cosmopolitan instinct ; that which allowed him to sympathise with Trojans, women, children and slaves, which inspired him with the beautiful thought that " the whole earth is the good man's fatherland," which also prompted him to despise the life of civic duty and activity and to recommend, as Aristotle does, the secluded and contemplative life. The further development of this cosmopolitan spirit and its effect on the old civic religion will be noted below.

It has been necessary to dwell so long on Euripides, not only for the reasons mentioned above, but also because owing to the vogue that he won in his lifetime and that was greatly to increase after his death, he more than any other of the great men of letters must be regarded as the populariser of the new enlightenment.

Whether he individually exercised any immediate religious influence upon the popular religious mind, for good or for harm, is not easy to decide with precision ; for there were other exponents than he of the same freer and more advanced thought, which began to express itself early in the sixth century. As a result we are able to discern the religious view of human life and conduct, becoming what we should term more spiritual, more inward. The moral judgment begins to look to the soul or the inner principle ; the doctrine begins to be proclaimed that God as a spiritual power can read the heart of man and judges him by that ; that sin lies not in the external act alone ; that external ritualistic purity is of less avail than purity of soul. Such thoughts as these which could serve as the foundation-stones of a new religion and which helped to shape the later religious history of Europe were mainly a heritage from the speculation of the sixth century and were in the air of the fifth. We cannot think that they were confined to the philosophic circles until Euripides gave them publicity ; for the notable oracle quoted and commented on by Herodotus had proclaimed to the people the novel view that a sinful purpose was the same in the sight of God as a sinful act ;[1] Epicharmos, the Sicilian poet of the earlier fifth century, had preached the higher ideal of purity—" if thou art pure in mind, thou art pure in thy whole body." It was probably in the latter part of the same century that some rhetorician of the school of Gorgias interpolated the proem of Hesiod's *Works and Days*, which reveals an exalted view of the High God.[2]

We may believe, then, that this higher religious ethic had a certain elevating influence on the popular imagination. The question of immediate interest is whether we can trace any effects of this in actual worship. Did the new enlightenment, for instance,

---

[1] 6, 86.

[2] Vide Ziegler, in *Archiv. f. Religionswiss*, 1911, p. 393–405.

lead to the abolition or reform of cruel or impure
or absurd forms of ritual ?

Human sacrifice.—This question involves the
consideration of the practice of human sacrifice,
which had been certainly prevalent in prehistoric
and early historic Greece, as in other Mediterranean
communities. We have evidence that in the fifth
and fourth centuries the practice was of rare occur-
rence in the Greek societies and was repugnant to the
religious morality of all but the most backward.
The feeling about the sacrifice of Iphigeneia mani-
fested in the Agamemnon of Æschylus, the story
about the Bœotian generals and the sacrifice of a
maiden before the battle of Leuktra are sufficient
proof.[1] The Platonic dialogue of the Minos contrasts
the Greeks with the barbarians in this matter,[2] yet
implies that the Arcadians in the cult of Zeus
Lykaios and the men of Halos in that of Zeus
Laphystios[3] continued the cruel offerings that
disgraced their Hellenism. Euripides attests that
the human sacrifice once customary in the rites of
Artemis, near Brauron, had been, before his day,
transformed to a mere fiction,[4] and at some time
earlier than this the Athenians must have ceased
to immolate human scapegoats, called φαρμακοί,
in their Thargelia.[5] The Rhodians eased their
consciences and at the same time maintained their
immemorial rite by choosing a malefactor who had
been condemned to death as a human victim to
Kronos.[6] According to Porphyry the practice

---

[1] Plut., *Vit. Pelop.*, C. 21, 22. Cf. Eur., *Iph. Taur.*, l. 391.
[2] p. 315 B–C.
[3] Cf. Herod., 7, 197, who shows that the human sacrifice in
this cult was rare and conditional.   [4] *Iph. Taur.*, l. 1458.
[5] Vide *Cults*, 4, pp. 276–279.   [6] Porphyry, *De Abstin.*, 2, 54.

survived here and there under the Roman Empire until the time of Hadrian.[1] And Plutarch[2] declares that the yearly custom of exposing the two Locrian maidens to the chance of a cruel death on the shore of Ilium, in expiation of the sin of Aias the Less against Athena Ilias, had been abandoned not very long before his time.

But the better sentiment of Greece in respect of such rites had probably begun to work as early as the time of Homer, for certain legends concerning the abolition of this ritual and the substitution of the animal for the human life point back to the prehistoric period ; and the merciful reform was ascribed to the High God himself in a Laconian legend that closely resembles the story of the sacrifice of Isaac.[3] The humanitarian spirit, then, had asserted itself before the sixth century ; but doubtless the higher teaching and thinking of this and the succeeding age quickened its influence.

Phallic ritual.—As regards that element in Greek ritual which the modern taste pronounces impure, there is little trace of any attempt at reform in any period of the polytheism. The element was indeed but slight. The forms of worship were, on the whole, decorous, often stately and beautiful ; ancient legend reveals the anxious care of the early Hellenes to preserve their temples from any sexual defilement ; where a ἱερὸς γάμος, or Holy Marriage, was enacted in any of the shrines, there is no need to suspect any licentiousness ;[4] no such feature is discernible in the Eleusinian or other Hellenic mysteries, although

---

[1] *Ib.*, 2, 56.   [2] De ser. num. vind., 12, p. 557 C–D.
[3] Plut., *Parallela*, 35. Vide *Cults*, 1, 95.
[4] Vide my *Greece and Babylon*, p. 267.

the Christian fathers are eager in their insinuations ;
the Hellenic[1] cults of the Oriental Aphrodite were
generally innocent of that ritual of temple-prostitu-
tion which was found in certain Anatolian cults and
which scandalised the Greek as much as the Christian
writers ; the few impure titles attaching to this
goddess may well have arisen in the later period of
the decadent polytheism.[2] In the early ages, it is
clear, the wholesome and temperate influence of the
Hellenic spirit had worked upon the forms of the
polytheism.   Nevertheless, in the ritual of a few
divinities, Demeter, Hermes, Dionysos, and even of
Artemis herself,[3] sexual emblems were occasionally in
vogue, dances of a more or less licentious character are mentioned, though these were very rare ;
while in the Thesmophoria and other services of
Demeter, what was called αἰσχρολογία, indecent and
scurrilous badinage, was indulged in by the women
among themselves or more rarely with the men
also.   We note that such ritual is practically confined to vegetation-cults, and in some it is merely
vegetation magic hardly attaching to the divinity,
nor affecting his or her moral aspect.   The phallic
emblem and the procession called the φαλλαγωγία
or φαλλοφορία were specially associated with
Dionysos and Hermes ;   and Plutarch, a man of
more than the average culture and refinement and
strikingly susceptible to the spiritual influences of
the more mystic religions, describes it as a harmless
adjunct of the ancestral and cheerful ritual of the

[1] The exceptions are the cults of Aphrodite at Corinth and
among the Lokri Epizephyrii.   Vide *Cults*, 2, pp. 635–636.
[2] *Cults*, 2, p. 667.
[3] e.g., in the cult of Artemis κορδάκα in Elis, said to be of
Lydian origin (*Cults*, Vol. II, p. 445).

Bœotian peasant.[1] Now it is worth noting that
against this element in Greek ritual there is scarcely
a word of protest in all the ethical and philosophic
literature of Greece. The exception is only a
fragmentary utterance of Herakleitos, in which he
seems to rail against the phallic procession of
Dionysos ; but the exact sense of his words is not
quite clear.[2] The higher moral thought of Greece
on this matter is probably more nearly represented
in the utterance of Aristotle in the Politics,[3] where
he lays down austere rules for the training of the
young : "No impure emblem or painting or any
representation of impropriety is to be allowed by
the archons, except in the cults of those divinities to
whom the law attaches the ritual of scurrility
($\tau\omega\theta\alpha\sigma\mu\acute{o}s$) : in their case the law allows those of
more advanced age to perform the divine service in
behalf of themselves, their children and their wives."
Even in the last three centuries before Christ, when
greater stress was continually being laid upon purity
in cult, no protest is heard against these old-world
forms, which have maintained themselves in many
parts of Europe down to the present day in spite of
the denunciations of Christianity. The seeming
paradox is explained when we reflect that the idea
of purity changes its content in the different generations ; and secondly that the Hellenic, like all the
other Mediterranean religions, except the Hebraic,
regarded the physical procreative power as belonging
to the divine character and as part of his cosmic
creative force ; therefore an emblem that was
secularly impure might be made holy by cult and
consecration. It is in this respect that the modern

---

[1] p. 527 D.   [2] Bywater, *Frag.*, CXXVII.   [3] 7, 17, p. 1336 *b*.

ideas of refinement differ most markedly from the classic.

Survival of other primitive ritual.—There is much besides in old Greek ritual that appears to us harmless but uncouth and irrational; strange and naïve things were done that primitive ideas of magic and animism inspired; and one may be surprised to find that the higher culture of the fifth and succeeding centuries is not known to have suppressed a single one of these. Still, in the time of Theophrastos, and indefinitely later, the Athenians were capable of the quaint old-world ritual of the Bouphonia, that strange medley of worship and magic and dramatic make-belief [1]; still in the time of Demosthenes [2] they were capable of bringing up to judgment in the law court an axe or any other inanimate thing that had caused the death of a man or of the sacred ox and solemnly condemning it to be thrown into the sea; the driving out of sin or famine, incarnate in a human being, was a ceremony in vogue at Massilia [3] and probably also at Athens long after the beginning of our era. Nor did the higher anthropomorphism, powerful as its working was, entirely obliterate the worship or half-worship of animals in the later centuries. [4] Even Zeus might still be conceived by the men of the fourth century as occasionally incarnate in the snake; and in a ritual law regulating the cult of Asclepios at Athens, composed shortly after 400 B.C., a sacrifice was ordered to certain sacred dogs; the pious votary would comply, however the act might awaken the laughter of a comic poet. Herakleitos protested against the

---

[1] *Cults*, I, pp. 56, 88–92.   [2] 23, § 76.
[3] Serv. ad Verg., *Æn.*, 3, 57.
[4] Vide my *Greece and Babylon*, pp. 76–81.

absurdity of praying to idols ; but no voice of the new enlightenment is heard against these far more irrational and backward ceremonies. The average public thought of the fifth century did not repudiate the use of magic ; in fact, it is not till the fifth century that its efficacy is known to have been recognised by legislation.[1] And Plato,[2] speaking about it in his Laws, a work of his declining years and intellect, is not sure whether he believes or disbelieves in its power. There is nothing more conservative than ritual ; and Greece produced no ardent Protestant reformer. Therefore, the average educated Athenian even of the fourth century would doubtless agree with the orator Lysias, that " it is prudent to maintain the same sacrifices as had been ordained by our ancestors who made our city great, if for no other reason, for the sake of the city's luck."[3]

Strength of the traditional religion in the fifth century.—The question naturally occurs—were the mass of the citizens touched at all in their inward theory of things by the spirit of modernism which breathed from Ionia and inspired the sophists ? The culture that was the stock-in-trade of the latter was only offered to those who could pay ; and upon these the poorer Athenian looked askance. He heard of it at first with a dislike that might become dangerous. Fanaticism, as we are familiar with it in the pages of European and Semitic history, was happily alien to the Greek temperament. But the banishment of Anaxagoras and Protagoras, and the execution of Sokrates by the city that was to become

---

[1] Vide fifth-century inscription of Teos containing a law threatening with penalties those who used magic against the State or against individuals (Rœhl, *Inscr. Græc. Antiq.*, 497).
[2] p. 932 E–933 E.   [3] *Or.*, 30, § 18.

the schoolmistress of Greece, might seem to savour somewhat of this temper of mind. These acts, indeed, were not inspired solely by religious feelings ; but they are clear proofs that the polytheism was by no means moribund and could be dangerous in its own defence. Nothing is more erroneous than the view which is sometimes expressed, that the popular devotion to the old religion was abating and its divine personalities and forms losing life and value towards the close of the fifth century. In their dark days the Athenians bided truer to their old faith than did Rome in her time of terror. We do not find a prostrate Athens turning desperately for aid to alien Oriental cults. We hear indeed of the beginnings of Adonis-cult in the latter part of the Peloponnesian war, the first ripple of a wave of Orientalism that was to surge westward later. But this feminine excess was unauthorised, and Aristophanes hates it and mocks at it. And the shallow view mentioned above would be sufficiently refuted by his comedy of ' the Clouds,' in which he, the greatest literary genius of his time, poses as the champion of the reaction against modernism. It is refuted also by other incidents in Athenian history that fall within the last decades of this century ; for the rage of the people at the mutilation of the Hermai, at the supposed insult to the Eleusinian mysteries, at the neglect of the dead after the battle of Arginousai, may be evidence of morbid religiosity, and is surely inconsistent with a general prevalence of scepticism. In these episodes the whole people reveal a passionate attachment to their holy mysteries, to their quaint phallic Herme-images on which the luck and the life of the State depended, to the duties of the loving tendance of the dead. Even their animistic beliefs concerning the common phenomena of the physical world had not yet been extirpated or purged by the physical philosophy of Ionia ; for according to Plato it was still a dangerous paradox, which his Sokrates disclaims before the jury, to maintain with Anaxagoras that the Sun and the Moon were merely material bodies and not in themselves divine. Intellectually Nikias appears inferior to Homer's Hektor. It was Athens that produced in the fourth century the ' superstitious man ' of Theophrastos ; but it is right to bear in mind that she also produced the man who could so genially and tolerantly expose that character.

Influence of comedy.—Those who believed that the faith in the polytheism was falling into rapid decay by 400 B.C. sometimes quote by way of evidence the astonishing licence of Attic comedy in dealing with the divine personalities ; the notorious example is the ludicrous figure and part of Dionysos in the Frogs of Aristophanes. Yet the people who enjoyed the humour of the play were more devoted to Dionysos than to most of the other persons of their pantheon. If the ' excellent fooling ' of Aristophanes is a proof of popular unbelief, what shall we say of that Attic terra-cotta of the sixth century that represents him half asleep and half drunk on the back of a mule and supported by an anxious Seilenos ?[1] The present writer has suggested that " this is some peasant's dedication, who feared his god little but loved him much and treated him *en bon camarade.*" Epicharmos in Sicily had been beforehand with Aristophanes in venturing on the burlesque of divine actions, Hephaistos and Herakles

[1] *Cults,* 5, p. 264.

specially lending themselves to ridiculous situations. Even in the epic period the same gay irreverence had occasionally appeared, as in the Homeric hymn to Hermes. These things do not necessarily arise from an anti-religious spirit, but they may be taken as indication of a certain vein in the Hellenic character, a light-heartedness and a reckless freedom in dealing on certain occasions with things divine that is markedly in contrast to the Oriental spirit. Nevertheless, it is not improbable that comedy at Athens and elsewhere did gradually exercise a weakening or a debasing influence on the popular faith. For the other poets of Attic comedy took greater liberties than even Aristophanes ; Kratinos and Telekleides of the fifth century, Amphis of the fourth, did not shrink from introducing the High God himself on the stage in ridiculous and licentious situations. There probably was some reserve and no gross indecency in the presentation of these plots. And much is conceded to the spirit of the carnival, especially when a certain αἰσχρολογία was sanctified by custom and ritual. Nevertheless, the more earnest-minded of the Athenians may have agreed with Plato's condemnation of such a handling of divine personages,[1] and though the popular faith may have been robust enough to endure such shocks, one cannot but suspect that the people's religious imagination suffered a debasement in moral tone. A few South-Italian vases of the fourth century, on which are scenes that appear to have been inspired by such comedies, are the worst examples of Hellenic vulgarity.

The history of Greek religion, then, must reckon with Attic comedy as among the possible causes of

---

[1] *Rep.*, 378 C., where he seems to glance at Epicharmos.

religious corruption and decay ; but at the worst this is only one side of the picture, for the fragments of the comedies of Menander, as will be shown, contain many a striking expression of the higher religious spirit and advanced ethical sentiment.

Waning of the political value of Delphi.—There are certain external events in the history of Greek religion towards the close of the fifth century that must be noted in a general sketch of its career. One is the waning of the political influence of the Delphic oracle ; its secular mission appeared to have been accomplished when the era of Greek colonial expansion had closed ; at the first terror of the Persian invasion the great states anxiously resorted to Delphi for guidance, but the priesthood failed to rise to the Pan-Hellenic occasion and played a double game. During the Peloponnesian war it was obvious that they were ' Laconising ' ; nor were they ever given again an opportunity of leading *la haute politique* of Hellas, and in the middle of the fourth century Demosthenes could speak contemptuously of ' the shadow at Delphi,' although the Amphictyonic League, as the only federal council of Hellas, still retained a nominal value sufficient to induce Philip to scheme for admission. Generally, in the fourth, third and second centuries, the oracle retained influence only in the spheres of religion and morality. Plato still regards the Delphic God as the natural director of the religious institutions of the State. And we have interesting examples in the later literature of consultation of the oracle by individuals whose minds were troubled by religious terrors and remorse. In fact, it came to serve the purposes of a private confessional, giving advice on questions of conscience ; and its advice was generally sane and often enlightened and shows the priests as possessed with the progressive spirit of Greek ethical philosophy.[1]

Spread of Asklepios-worship.—Another event of importance is the diffusion of the cult of Asklepios and the growing influence on the Hellenic mind of this once obscure hero or earth-daimon of the Thessalian Trikka. It was thence that sometime probably in the sixth century he had migrated to Epidauros, where his power expanded through his union with Apollo. His cult-settlement in Kos was connected with the Epidaurian ; and already in the fifth century the Asclepieion of this favoured island had reared the great Hippokrates and was thus the cradle of the later medical science of Europe. Towards the close of this century Asklepios and his daughters came even from Epidauros to Athens, and according to a well-founded tradition the poet Sophocles was his first apostle ; in the next generation we find the Athenian state regulating his worship, which was soon to conquer the whole Hellenic world. And in the survey of the Hellenistic age it must be reckoned with as one of the main religious forces of later Hellenism. We may note in passing a striking divergence between the European spirit of Hellenic religion and the Oriental spirit of Mesopotamia : the Babylonian God practises magic, the Hellenic Asklepios, though he worked miracles enough, came in a later day at least to foster science, and even his cases at Epidauros were not all merely of the Lourdes type.

Growth of the Thiasoi.—Another interesting phenomenon that begins to arrest our attention in

I   [1] Vide *Cults,* 4, pp. 211–214.

the latter part of the fifth century is the growth of private θίασοι or voluntary religious associations independent of the public religion and devoted to a special divinity who might be an alien. The most interesting testimony is the title of a comedy by Eupolis called the ' Baptai,' which we may interpret as 'the Baptisers,' satirising a society devoted to the Thracian goddess, Kotytto, whose initiation-rites must have included a ceremony of baptism, of which this is the earliest example within the Hellenic area. It will be more convenient to estimate the importance of religious significance of these θίασοι in the survey of the next period of our history. Meanwhile, it is well to mark certain evidence that the most powerful and appealing of these, the Orphic mystery, having failed in the sixth century to capture the States of Magna Græcia, was increasing its private influence in Eastern Greece in the century before the rise of Alexander. Plato's attack is itself a witness of this. And when Aristophanes[1] and an Attic orator contemporary with Demosthenes[2] openly acknowledge Orpheus as the apostle to the Hellenes of the most holy mysteries, and the teacher of a higher way of life, we must conclude that the spirit of the Orphic brotherhoods had touched the imagination of the general public outside the circle of the initiated.

Religion in first half of fourth century B.C.—Yet it is hazardous and probably false to say that the public religion of Greece was decaying visibly throughout the first half of the fourth century. Athens is as usual our chief witness. The restored democracy was all the more strenuous in matters of religion as scepticism was considered a mark of the

[1] *Frags.*, 1032.　　　　[2] κ. 'Αριστογειτ, § 11.

new culture of the oligarchically-minded. The trial
of Socrates is an indication of this temper. We have
also evidence from this period of the occasional
severity of the Athenian people against those who
tried to introduce unauthorised and un-Hellenic
cults. The Hellenic tradition is still strong against
the contagion of the orgiastic spirit of the Anatolian
religion, and it was with difficulty that the Athenian
public could tolerate the wild ritual of Sabazios
and the Phrygian Mother, nor even in the time of
Demosthenes were the participants in it secure from
danger. The early fourth-century art still exhales
the religious spirit and serious ethos of the Pheidian
school ; and it created the type, and almost suc-
ceeded in establishing the cult, of the new Goddess
of Peace, Eirene, for whose presence among them
the wearied Athenians might well yearn ; it also
perfected the ideal of Demeter, the Madre Dolorosa
of Greek myth, whose Eleusinian rites with their
benign promise of salvation added power and
significance to the later polytheism. The literature
of this period attests the enduring vitality of the
popular religion. The Attic oratory of the fourth
century was more religious in its appeal than any
modern has been, as might be expected of a time
when there was yet no divorce conceivable between
Church and State. It is not a question of the
religious faith of the individual orator, but of the
religious temper of the audience which is attested
by many striking passages in the speeches. According to Antiphon, the punishment of sinners and the
avenging of the wronged is specially the concern of
the deities of the nether world[1] ; Andokides avers

[1] *Or.*, 1, p. 31.

that foul misconduct was a more heinous sin in a man who had been in the service of the Mother and the Maid of Eleusis[1] ; the speech against Aristogeiton is almost as much a religious as a juridical utterance. Demosthenes may have been a sceptic at heart, believing in chance—as he once says—as the governing force of our life ; but otherwise he is glowingly orthodox in respect of Attic religion and mythology, and the greatest of his speeches closes with a fervent and pious prayer.[2]   And again it is well to remind ourselves that the political or forensic orator is a truer witness to the average popular belief than the poet or the philosopher.

Plato's attitude towards the popular religion.—A consecutive history of Greek religious thought as embodied in the surviving writings or records of the philosophic schools of Hellas is far too large a subject even to be adumbrated here. And a general survey of the religion can only notice shortly the leading thinkers whose works there is reason to suppose had popular vogue and lasting influence upon the religious world.

Among these the primacy belongs to Plato ; and the full account of Greek religion, both in the period that precedes the downfall of Greek independence and in the periods that follow, must include a critical estimate of his religious speculation. This is no place for an elaborate consideration of the metaphysic of his ideal theory, or the relation of his ideas to a theistic system ; but only the most general observations may be allowed for the purpose of this sketch. To understand his main attitude towards the popular cults, and his influence upon the later

[1] *De Myster.*, § 125 ; cf. § 31.   [2] *De Cor.*, § 324.

educated world of Greece, we must recognise at once
that, idealist and reformer as he was, he was no
revolutionary or iconoclast in matters of religion ;
he would reform Greek mythology, purging it of
stories of divine conflicts, divine vengeance, divine
amours ; and, as these fortunately were enshrined
in no sacred books, he feels that this might be done
gently and easily without disturbance to the established forms of worship.   He does not desire to
abolish sacrifice or idolatry, but inculcates simplicity
in the offerings.[1]   In one passage he even maintains
that the legislator will not change a single detail of
the ritual, if only for the reason that he does not
know anything of the inner truth that may lie
behind such outward forms.[2]   Even in his most
advanced physical and metaphysical speculations
he finds a place for the popular pantheon ;[3] in the
hierarchic scale of things the Olympians are ranged
somewhere below the supreme transcendental God
of the Universe.   The ' Timæus ' dialogue presents
some interesting theologic dogma ; here[4] in the scale
of Divine creation the Olympian Pantheon, which
seems to be accepted rather for the sake of ancient
tradition, is given the third place after the planets
and the Sun which are the second works of the
Supreme Creator, the first being the cosmic Heaven.
These deities of the polytheism, then, are not
immortal in their own nature, but are held together
for all eternity by the will of the highest God.   And
it was to them that he committed the formation of
man, and lent for this purpose a portion of his own
immortality ; the mortality of man is thus accounted

---

[1] *Laws*, 956 A–B.   [2] *Ib.*, 985 D.
[3] e.g. *ib.*, 984 D.   [4] p. 34–41.

for ; which would have been inexplicable had he sprung directly from the immortal Supreme Being.

It is interesting for our present purpose to note that this esoteric and transcendental system, devised by the great master and parent of Greek theosophy, would leave the established religion more or less unimpaired ; it even accepts its data at certain points, namely, the nativity of its Gods, and draws the logical conclusion that Gods, who were born could not be by essence immortal ; therefore Zeus could not be accepted as the Absolute and Supreme Being of the Cosmos. Also it proclaims the idea of an immortal element in man, which, again, is in accord not only with Orphic teaching, but also with the contemporary popular faith in the survival of some part of our being after death. But the work which reflects most vividly the popular religion and betrays the strongest sympathy with it is the Laws, a work of his old age in which the conservative spirit of the religious reformer is no less striking than the intellectual decay of the philosopher. He accepts the greater part of the civic political religion, merely purifying the mythology and some of the ideas concerning divinity ; and it is striking how easily he finds in it materials ready to his hand on which he can build an exalted ethical-religious system of rights and duties, especially those which concern the life of the family and the groups of kinship.[1] In fact, the background of the thought in this lengthy treatise is almost always the Greek Polis, though glimpses may here and there break through of a wider vista. He expresses the prejudices of the Greek citizen against new forms of private or foreign orgiastic cult which

[1] For particulars vide *Hibbert Lectures*, pp. 37, 46–48, 103, 117.

were dangerously enticing to women ;[1] any doubtful question that might arise concerning rite or cult he would leave to the decision of the oracles of Delphi or Dodona or of Zeus Ammon.[2] We feel generally that Plato did not assume the part of an apostle of a new order of religion, but that both in his philosophy and religious theory he found a sufficient *point d'appui* in the old, of which he tried to strengthen the moral potentialities.

The later sects which attached themselves to his name or to his school were deeply interested in religious speculation, which degenerates at last into the mystic superstition of Neoplatonism. Therefore, as the work of Aristotle belongs to the history of European science, so the philosophy of Plato concerns the later history, both of pre-Christian and Christian religious thought. To estimate exactly how his influence worked on the better popular mind in the centuries before Christ is impossible. But we may naturally and with probability surmise that he contributed much to the diffusion of the belief in the spiritual nature and perfection of God, to the extirpation of the crude notions of divine vindictiveness and jealousy, to the interpretation of the external world in terms of mind and spirit as against any materialistic expression, to the acceptance of the belief in the divinity of the human soul and its affinity with God and in the importance of its posthumous life, which was partly conditioned by the attainment of purity. These latter ideas constitute the faith of the Orphic sects, from whom Plato may have silently borrowed them. But whether through Plato or the thiasoi many of them

[1] *Laws*, p. 909 E.   [2] 738 C.

came to appeal strongly to the popular mind of later Hellas.

Religious art in the fourth century.—Our general survey is now approaching that period of world-change brought about by the rise of Macedon. But before leaving the scene of the free City-State, we should remember to estimate the religious work done by the great fourth-century masters of sculpture before the power of Alexander reached its zenith. The fiery imagination of Skopas found plastic types for the forms of Dionysos and his thiasos, and his work rivalled at least, if it did not surpass, in inspiration of tumultuous life the masterpieces of the older Attic vase-painters noticed above. Praxiteles, the master of the gentler moods of the soul, in the religious sphere consummated the types of Aphrodite and Demeter ; the almost perfect embodiment of the latter goddess, the Cnidian Demeter of the British Museum, a work of his school, combines something of the tearful expression of the Madre Dolorosa with the blitheness of the Corn-Goddess. We are conscious indeed of a change in the representation of divinity. The works of this later generation have lost the majesty and awe, the σεμνότης, as the Greeks called it, of the fifth-century art ; nor can the Greek states command any longer the creation of the chryselephantine colossal statues of temple-worship. In these later types, though still divine, there is more infusion of human passion, of the personal experience, the struggles and yearning of the individual soul. Anthropomorphism is pursuing its path, and though still fertile in works of high spiritual value, may come to weary and weaken the religious sense.

CHAPTER V

THE PERIOD AFTER ALEXANDER

THE establishment of the Macedonian Empire wrought momentous changes in the civic-political religion of Hellas ; and some of these were in the direction of loss and decay, while others worked for the birth of new religious life. The political significance of Apollo of Delphi, of Zeus and Athena, the divine leaders of the Polis in its counsels and ambitions, was doomed to pass away. Athena, as the warder and counsellor, was of less avail for Athens than were the Samothracian sea-deities for the victorious Demetrios.

Certainly in the first centuries of the Hellenistic age there were few external signs of decay ; we do not yet hear of ruined shrines or the decline of great festivals such as the Delia ; Athena, though no longer the goddess of a civic Empire, was still and for ages yet remained the benign Madonna for the Athenian, to whose care the boy-athlete and the marriageable girl were dedicated ; we have record from the island of Tenos[1] of the abiding hold that even such a deity as Poseidon still exercised on the affections of his people, as late as the second and first centuries B.C. ; and if we had continuous chronicles of each cult-centre we should probably find similar evidence showing that the dominant

[1] *Bull. Corr. Hell.*, XXVI, pp. 399–489.

figures of the old polytheism were still able to fulfil
in some degree the religious wants of the individual
worshipper.   And scholars who have been tempted
to ante-date the decay of Hellenic polytheism have
ignored, among other evidence, this important
historic fact that in the fourth century it was still
vital enough to make foreign conquests, to penetrate and take possession of Carthage, for instance,
and that in the third century it began to secure for
itself a new lease of life within the city and the
growing Empire of Rome ; in fact, the last chapter
of Greek religion falls within the Roman imperial
period.

Growing force of personal religion.—Yet the
Hellene in the fourth century and in the early days
of Macedonian ascendancy began to crave other
outlets for his religious emotion than the traditional
cults of his phratry or tribe or city.   Personal
religion was beginning to be a more powerful impulse
and to stimulate a craving in the individual for a
more intimate union with the divinity, such, for
instance, as was offered freely by the Great Mysteries
of Eleusis.   And we have fairly sufficient evidence
that the fourth century witnessed a great extension
of their influence.[1]   The mysteries of Megalopolis
were instituted and those of Andania were reorgan-
ised by their aid ; and the first Ptolemy is said
to have invited an apostle from Eleusis to assist
in some religious institutions of his new city of
Alexandria.[2]

The religious brotherhoods.—The same aspiration
was also satisfied by the private θίασοι, the guilds
of brethren devoted to the special cult of one

---

[1] Vide *Cults*, 3, pp. 199–202.   [2] *Ib.*, p. 199.

divinity. These unions belong to the type of the secret religious society which is found in all parts of the world at varying levels of culture. In Greece we have evidence of them as early as the time of Solon ; it was probably not till the fifth century that any of them were instituted for the service of foreign divinities ; we hear then of the thiasos of the Thracian Goddess, and in the earlier half of the fourth century of the orgiastic fraternity devoted to Sabazios, with which Æschines in his youth was associated. But it is not till the Macedonian period that the epigraphic record of them begins ; henceforth the inscriptions are numerous and enlightening concerning their organisation and their wide prevalence throughout the Hellenic world.[1] Their importance for the history of religion is great on various grounds.

They show the development of the idea of a humanitarian religion in that they transcend, in most cases, the limits of the old tribal and civic religion and invite the stranger ; so that the members, both men and women, associate voluntarily, no longer on the ground of birth or status, but drawn together by their personal devotion to a particular deity, to whom they stand in a far more intimate and individual relation than the ordinary citizen could stand to the divinities of his tribe and city. This sense of divine fellowship might sometimes have been enhanced by a sacrament which the members partook of together ; we know that this was the bond of fellowship in the Samothracian mysteries, which were beginning to appeal widely to the early Hellenistic world. A common meal at

---

[1] Vide Foucart, *Des Associations religieuses.*

least, a love-feast or ' Agape,' formed the chief bond
of the ' thiasotai,' and this was sometimes a funeral-
feast commemorative of the departed brother or
sister. There was nothing to prevent the thiasos
choosing as its patron-deity some one of the leading
divinities of traditional polytheism, to which they
must not be supposed, as Foucart supposed them,
to stand in any natural antagonism ; therefore, for
instance, there were local reasons why Greek
merchants whose central meeting-point was Rhodes
should form θίασοι under the protection and in the
name of Zeus Xenios, the God who protects the
stranger, or of Athena Lindia, the ancient and
powerful divinity of Lindos, or of Helios, the
prehistoric Sun-God whose personality pervaded the
whole island. So far, then, the religious importance
of these societies consists in their quickening influence on personal religion, in the gratification that
they afforded to the individuals craving for personal
union with the Godhead, also in their organisation
which aroused a keener sense of religious fellowship
between the members, and which later served as a
model to the nascent Christian community. But in
the history of the Hellenic religion their significance
is even greater on another ground, namely, that
they bear a most striking testimony to that fusion
of East and West which it was the object of Alexander, and the mission of his successors, to effect ;
for many of these religious brotherhoods, whose
members and organisation were Hellenic, were
consecrated to foreign deities, Sabazios, Adonis,
Xousares, the Syrian Goddess ; so that they
played undesignedly the part of missionaries in
the momentous movement sometimes called the

Θεοκρασία, the blending of Eastern and Western religions and divine personalities, of which the significance will be considered a little later.

Menander.—The student who is tracking the course of the religious life and experience of Hellas through the Hellenistic period should endeavour to gather beforehand a vivid impression of the spirit of the Menandrian comedy. For Menander, the friend of Epicurus and the devoted admirer of Euripides, was the favoured heir of the humanitarian spirit that had gleamed fitfully even in the Homeric period and had gathered strength and articulate expression in the century before Alexander opened the gates of the East. Patronised and courted by Demetrios Phalereus and Ptolemy, admired by the scholars and reading public of Alexandria and the Hellenistic world even more than he had been by his own contemporaries, Menander was eminently in a position to give a tone to the religious sentiment of this period ; and the Anthologies of his works prove that he was actually reverenced as an ethical-religious teacher.[1] Therefore, for the general exoteric history of Greek religion he counts for more than any of the philosophers, for he addressed a far larger public. Yet the message that he has to deliver has come to him from the philosophers and from the inspiration of the humanised Attic spirit, of which he appears

---

[1] A paper by Pierre Waltz in the *Revue des Études Grecques,* 1911—'sur les sentences de Ménandre'—aims at discovering or imagining the dramatic setting of each fragment and at disproving the view that Menander was posing as an original ethical teacher. Accepting his theory, we can still assign high value to the 'sentences' for the purpose of Greek ethical history, whether we regard them as original and earnest utterances of Menander or commonplaces which he uses lightly for dramatic purposes ; for if the latter view of them is the truer, they show at least what was in the air.

the most delicate and final expression. While writing and thinking pre-eminently as the cultured Athenian of the close of the fourth century, he is the mouthpiece of cosmopolitanism in ethics and religion—" no good man is alien to me ; the nature of all is one and the same (οὐδείς ἐστί μοι ἀλλότριος ἂν ἦ χρηστός· ἡ φύσις μία πάντων) "[1] ; the Terentian formula—' homo sum, humanum nil a me alienum puto '—is only an extension of this, losing something of its ethical colouring. Many of the fragments, showing striking approximations to New Testament teaching, are of vital importance for the history of Greek ethics. As regards religion, they may contain protests against superstition and the extravagance of sacrifice proffered as a bribe[2] ; but they exhibit no real or veiled attack on the popular polytheism as a whole. On the other hand, they have preserved many memorable sentences that bear witness to the development of a religion more personal, more inward and spiritual than had hitherto been current, save perhaps in Platonic circles. God is presented as a spirit and as spiritually discerned by the mind of man ; and a high ideal of Platonic speculation is delivered to the public in the beautiful line, φῶς ἐστὶ τῷ νῷ πρὸς θεὸν βλέπειν ἀεί, " the light of the mind is to gaze ever upon God."[3] The sense of close and mystic communion between man and the divine omnipresent spirit is strikingly attested in the passage of one of his unknown comedies : " a guardian spirit [δαίμων] stands by every man, straightway from his birth,

---

[1] Kock, *Com. Att. Frag.*, 602.
[2] e.g., quotation by Clemens, *Strom,* p. 720 P. Cf. fragment of the Ἱέρεια, Kock, 245.
[3] Γνῶμαι Μονοστιχ, 589, Meineke, 4, p. 356.

to guide him into the mysteries of life, a good spirit, for one must not imagine that there is an evil spirit injuring good life, but that God is utterly good."[1]

In attempting to grasp what is most elusive, the inner religious sentiment of any period, it is important to remember that the author of such expression was dear to at least the cultivated public of the Hellenistic age.

The Θεοκρασία.—The tolerant humanitarianism of Menander, of which we catch the echo in certain formulæ inscribed on the Delphic and other temples, is reflected in that which is perhaps the most striking religious phenomenon of this period, namely, the 'theocrasia,' the fusion of divinities of East and West. As regards religious theory this is not to be regarded as a new departure. Herodotus shows how natural it was to the Hellenic mind to interpret the deities of foreign nations in terms of its native pantheon ; and it was easy for Euripides to commend Kybele as Demeter.[2] But it was by no means easy, in fact it was exceedingly dangerous, before the time of Alexander, to introduce any unauthorised foreign cult into the City-State. We hear vaguely of the death-sentence inflicted or threatened on those who did so. Nevertheless, as we have seen, such foreigners as Sabazios and Attis were intruding themselves into Athens at the time of the Peloponnesian war, trailing with them the orgiastic atmosphere of Phrygia ; and at some indefinite time before this the impure ritual of certain Oriental Goddess-cults had invaded the Corinthian worship of Aphrodite. But after the establishment of the kingdoms of the Diadochi, the gentile barrier in

[1] *Fab. Incert.*, Kock, *Frag.*, 550. [2] Helene, 1300–1365.

religion loses gradually its force and significance. It was, in fact, a far-sighted measure of policy on the part of some of the kings to establish some common cult that might win the devotion of the Hellenic and Oriental peoples alike. Such was the intention of Ptolemy when he founded at Alexandria the cult of the Babylonian god, Sarapis, whom the Egyptians were able owing to a similarity of name to identify with their Osiris-Apis, and the Hellenes with their Plouton, owing to the accidental fact that an image of this underworld-god happened to be consecrated to the cult at its first institution. Similarly, when the Syrian city of Bambyke was resettled as Hierapolis by Seleukos Nikator, the personality of the great goddess, Atargatis, was blent with that of Artemis, Hera, Aphrodite and other Hellenic goddesses ; and the treatise of Lucian, *de Dea Syria*, gives us the most interesting picture presented by antiquity of the working of the θεοκρασία in the domain of religion and religious art.

The spirit of syncretism grows stronger and more pervading through the later Greek and Græco-Roman periods, and dominates the later Orphic and Gnostic thought ; and the inscriptions, usually the best record of the popular religious practice, attest its wide diffusion. We find the deities of diverse lands—Egypt, Syria and Greece—linked together in the same formula of thanksgiving and the same offering dedicated to them all. And the name Zeus is applied to so many gods of the East that in the cult-formulæ it seems often to have lost all its personal and concrete value and acquired the vaguer meaning of ' God.' The Jewish Jahivé himself—under the name ᾽Ιάω—was occasionally identified with him and at times, it seems, even with Dionysos.[1]

The importance of this movement for religious thought was of the highest. Varro's view, recorded by Augustine.[2] that the name of the deity made no difference, so long as ' the same thing is understood,' and that therefore the God of the Jews was the same as Jupiter, is a great idea that has been bequeathed to the world by Greek tolerance and Greek sanity. Only a nation could attain to this freedom of religious imagination that was not held captive by the magic spell of names[3] which made it so difficult for the Jew to shake off the tribal spirit of the religious blood-feud. This Hellenic expression of religious enlightenment prepared the way for monotheism and thus indirectly for Christianity. It also could induce the pantheistic idea of a diffused omnipresent spirit of divinity, such as is expressed in the lines of Aratos, the scientific poet of the third century B.C., " all the ways are full of (the spirit of) God, and all the gathering-places of men, the sea and harbours ; and at every turn we are all in need of God,[4] for we are of kin to him."

Stoicism, Epicureanism, Cynicism.—This pantheistic speculation inspires some of the dogmas of Stoicism ; and for most of the Stoic writers and thinkers the concept of divinity was less that of a personal concrete Being than of a spiritual force or soul-power immanent in things ; therefore while some of them tried to find a place in their

---

[1] Vide A. B. Cooke, *Zeus*, pp. 232–234.
[2] *De Consensu Evangelistarum*, 1, 30 (**xxii**) ; **of. *De Civ. Dei.*,** IV, 9.
[3] Vide my *Hibbert Lectures*, pp. 104–106.
[4] Phainomen, 1, 2–5.

metaphysical system for the creations of the polytheism and even a justification for augury and
divination, the impression left on our minds by the
fragments that have come down to us of the religious
speculation of the Stoa is as of a system alien and
antipathetic to the popular theistic point of view
and especially to the social religion of kin-group and
city ; and Zeno the founder is said to have protested
against shrines and idols.[1] His protest was in vain ;
nor is there any clear indication that Stoicism had
any influence on the religious thought and practice
of the average man of the people ; unless, indeed,
the emergence of the cult of $Aρετή$, Virtue, in the
second century B.C. at Pergamon and Smyrna was
suggested by the strong theologic colouring that the
Stoics gave to morality.[2]

As for Epicureanism, it cannot be regarded
normally as a religious force ; if it touched the
popular mind at all its influence must have been
generally in the direction of atheism or indifferent-
ism ; the only signs that it did are occasional grave-
inscriptions that breathe the Epicurean spirit of
unperturbed quiescence in regard to the posthumous
fate of the soul.

The philosophic school that was most aggressively
protestant against the popular creeds and cults
appears to have been the Cynic, mordant and out-
spoken criticism being characteristic of this sect.
We have record of Diogenes' contempt for the
Eleusinian mysteries, of Antisthenes' disdain for the
Great Mother of Phrygia and her mendicant priests ;
and the fragments in a newly discovered papyrus of

[1] Clem., *Strom.*, p. 691.
[2] Vide *Cults*, 5, pp. 446, 745 R, 221.

a treatise by Kerkidas,[1] the Cynic philosopher and statesman of Megalopolis in the third century B.C., contain a theory which reduces personal deities to impotent instruments of Fate and would substitute for Zeus and his colleagues certain divinised abstractions, such as Nemesis and 'Μετάδως; the latter term, if the reading is sound, seems to denote the Spirit of Unselfishness or Sacrifice, an interesting and potentially valuable idea, but at this time still-born.

Asclepios-Cult and later mysteries.—The philosophic sectarians of this later age do not appear to have made a serious attempt to capture the mind of the public ; and the popular religious movements for the most part ignored them and their teaching. The Hellenistic religions are as convincedly theistic and idolatrous as the older were. The chief change lay in this, that a man now might to some extent choose his own divinity or—what was even of more import—be chosen by him or her ; he was no longer limited to the cults into which he was born. This freedom had already for some time been offered by the ' thiasoi ' ; and now in the Hellenistic world, especially through the powerful and wide influence of the cult of Asklepios, the idea was developed of a deity who as Healer and Saviour called all mankind to himself ; and it was this significant cult-phenomenon that induced Kerkidas in the above-mentioned passage to include Παιάν, the ' Healer,' among the true divinities whose worship ought to supplant that of the older gods. In the treatise called ' Asclepios ' of the pseudo-Apuleius a long address and prayer to this deity are preserved of which the tone is strikingly

[1] *Oxyrhynch. Papyri.*, viii, p. 31.

Christian.[1] " We rejoice in thy divine salvation, because thou hast shown thyself wholly to us ; we rejoice that thou hast deigned to consecrate us to eternity, while we are still in these mortal bodies. . . . We have known thee, oh, true life of the life of man. . . . Adoring thy goodness we make this our only prayer . . . that thou wouldst be willing to keep us all our lives in the love of thy knowledge."

Non-Hellenic mysteries.—The phenomenon here indicated attests the stronger vitality at this period of personal or individual, as distinct from tribal or political religion ; and this was quickened also by the growth of certain non-Hellenic mysteries in the Mediterranean area in the latter centuries of Paganism, notably by the Samothracian, those of Attis and the Great Mother, the Egyptian Isis, and finally in the last period of all of Mithras. In most of these the records allow us to discover many interesting ideas that reappear in early Christianity, such, for instance, as communion with the divinity through sacrament, the mystic death and rebirth of the Catechumen, the saving efficacy of baptism and purification. These rites could satisfy the craving of the mortal to attain to the conviction of immortality and to the ecstatic consciousness of complete or temporary self-absorption in God. But in the mysteries of Sabazios and Cybele and possibly in others this sense of divinity was conveyed to the ' mystes ' by the simulation of a holy marriage or sex-communion with the God or Goddess ; and for this reason the Pagan mysteries were generally attacked by the Christian Fathers as obscene ; the

[1] Vide *Archiv, für Relig. Wiss.*, 1904, p. 395 ; my *Evolution of Religion*, p. 207.

charge was unjust on the whole, though the psychic effect of the special act of ritual just alluded to was probably detrimental to the moral imagination.

Hermetic literature.—The strangest and most interesting manifestation that the ancient records have preserved for us of this fusion of Hellenic culture and Oriental religious sentiment is presented by the Hermetic literature. The origins of this fantastic product of the human mind are traced by Professor Petrie[1] back to the sixth or fifth centuries B.C. But, though much of it is pre-Christian, its philosophic diction proves that it cannot be earlier than 300 B.C., and the bulk of it is probably later.[2] A frequent Hermetic formula, addressed to the deity —ἐγώ εἰμι σὺ καὶ σὺ ἐγώ, " I am Thou and Thou art I "—may be taken as the master-word of these hieratic writings. This unnatural alliance between Greek philosophy and Oriental mystic theosophy is a momentous phenomenon of later Paganism ; and the study of the origins of Christian metaphysic is much concerned with it.

Such theosophy had a natural affinity with magic ; and magic, always a power in an age of intellectual decay, begins to be most powerful in this latest age of Hellenism. It is a just reproach that Augustine brings against Porphyry, the most notable of the Neoplatonists that he ' wavered between philosophy and a sacrilegious curiosity,' that is, a vicious interest in the black art.[3]

In these strange forms of faith and speculation the clearness and sanity of the pure Hellenic intellect appear clouded and troubled, the lineaments of the

---

[1] *Personal Religion in Egypt*, p. 40.
[2] Vide Reitzenstein, *Poimandres.*   [3] *De Civ. Dei.*, 10, 9.

old types of the Hellenic thought and imagination almost effaced. And the learning and science of the Hellenistic age stood mainly aloof from the religious forces that moved the masses of the people.

Daimonism.—The mystic and theosophic literature of the Hellenistic and Græco-Roman period was markedly 'daimonistic,' being infected with the polydaimonism of the East and positing the existence of good and evil 'daimones' as a metaphysic dogma. We can trace a corresponding change in the popular Hellenic imagination. In the earlier period, as has been shown, the native Hellene was, as compared with other races, fairly strong-minded in respect of the terrors of the demon-world ; but the later people of the Greek area were certainly tainted in some degree with this unfortunate superstition of the East, and various forms of exorcism, conjuration and evocation became more prevalent. The modern Greek temperament appears to be morbidly possessed with this disease[1] ; and we may suppose that the germs have been inherited and developed from this last period of the old civilisation.

Eschatology.—But another feature that we mark in these mystic worships and mystic societies of the Hellenistic world indicates a higher aspect of religion and marks an epoch in religious aspiration. Most of them, if not all, proclaimed the immortality of the soul, a happy resurrection, a divine life after death. The Hellene who had been initiated into the Osiris faith hoped to attain immortal happiness in and through Osiris, availing himself of Egyptian ideas and Egyptian spell-formulæ. The priest of certain

[1] Vide J. C. Lawson, *Modern Greek Folklore and Ancient Greek Religion*, 1910.

mysteries, probably of Attis, comforts the congregation of the faithful, sorrowing over the death of their
God, with words that aver the certainty of his
resurrection and by implication the hope of their
own—

> θαρρεῖτε μύσται τοῦ θεοῦ σεσωσμένου
> ἔσται γὰρ ἡμῖν ἐκ πόνων σωτηρία.[1]

" Be of good cheer, ye of the mystery of the saved
God, for after our troubles there shall be to us
salvation."

The mysteries of Mithras embodied much the
same eschatologic ideas and hopes ; but these came
to the Græco-Roman world only in the latest period
before the establishment of Christianity, and had
little hold on Hellenic society proper. Doubtless the
most attractive mystery for the Hellenes was the
Orphic, and we have many proofs of its activity and
life in the two centuries before and after the beginning of our era ; and we can well understand the
causes of its popularity. Its deity had become
Hellenised long ago ; the Orphic formulæ were free
from barbarous jargon and admitted the familiar
divine names ; the insistence on purification was
congenial to many Hellenic temperaments ; there
was probably nothing surviving in the ritual that was
objectionable to the cultivated Hellene ; and finally
its picture of Paradise seems to have accorded with
the trend of the Hellenic imagination. The numerous grave-inscriptions of these centuries rarely
express any definite Orphic sentiment or allude to
any specially mystic faith ; but we know that the

---

[1] Firm. Mat., *De Err.*, 22 ; cf. Dieterich, *Eine Mithras-
Liturgie,* p. 174.

sacred hymn of the votaries was buried with them from the fourth century down to the Roman Imperial period ; and we have the evidence of Plutarch attesting the prevalence of these societies and their power of appeal, for, when he is consoling his wife for the death of their child, he reminds her of the promises of future happiness held out by the Dionysiac mysteries, into which they have both been initiated.[1]

Hero-worship and apotheosis.—The idea that was common to many of these mystic brotherhoods, that the mortal might achieve divinity, is illustrated by another religious phenomenon which stands out in this latest period, namely, the worship of individual men and women either in their lifetime or immediately after death. To appreciate the full significance of this, one must be familiar with the usages of the earlier Hellenes as also of the Oriental peoples who became subjects of the Diadochi. We have observed that the Greek of the sixth and fifth centuries was willing to concede heroic honours to certain distinguished individuals after death ; in this there was nothing inconsistent with the principles of higher polytheism ; and in the earlier cases the grounds of canonisation were usually good and reasonable. It becomes a more serious question about the religious and moral character of a people when divine worship is proffered to a living person. Of this the first example is the cult of Lysander as a God, which, as Plutarch seems to imply, arose even in his lifetime.[2] The same writer records the story of the apotheosis offered by the people of Thasos

---

[1] *Consol. ad uxor.*, 10, p. 611 D.
[2] Vit. Lysandr., 18. Cf. Athenag, p. 51 (Lechair).

to Agesilaos and his sarcastic refusal.[1] The same kind of adulation was lavished by the degenerate Athenians on Alexander and Demetrios Poliorketes. The most salient examples are derived from the records of the Seleukidai and the Ptolemies, the kings of these dynasties usually enjoying divine honours after death, and sometimes bearing divine titles, such as Σωτηρ, Saviour, Θεός, or God, in their lifetime. Is this merely the gross servility of a decadent age that had lost all real sense of religion ? This is no doubt the true account of it in some degree ; Dio Chrysostom exclaims against the quackery and vanity of it ;[2] and the sharp-witted Athenians and the educated Greek generally would be under no illusion when they prostrated themselves before these human-Gods. It is natural to suppose that the effect upon the life of the old religion was corrosive when a queen or a courtesan could be publicly recognised as Aphrodite, and that the general belief in Apollo and Dionysos would tend to collapse when the one was identified with the Seleukidai, the other with Attalos. Yet the faith in Dionysos at least was able to survive the strain. And what seems to us mere hypocrisy and blasphemy would appear to many of the Hellenistic communities in another light. It seems that the un-cultured Greek in the time of Herodotus was capable of believing in all seriousness that Xerxes might be a real incarnation of Zeus upon earth ;[3] and such an idea would be familiar, as an old tradition in the popular estimate of kingship, to the

---

[1] p. 210 D, *Apoth. Lacon ;* he advised them to begin with making themselves Gods if they felt equal to making him one.
[2] *Or.,* 64 R, 338 (Dind, 2, p. 213).   [3] 7, 56.

natives of Syria and still more to the Egyptians. When the Rosetta stone proclaims the Ptolemy as 'the living image of God,' the average Greek might smile in secret, but the native Egyptian would instinctively assent to this assumption of divinity by the heir of the ancient Pharaohs.

This apotheosis of the mortal, so rife in this later period, may be regarded as a moral and religious evil. Yet it must not be taken too hastily as a proof of the unreality of the prevailing polytheism. And, for better or worse, it was a momentous fact belonging to the higher history of European religion ; for it familiarised the Græco-Roman world with the idea of the incarnation of the Man-God.

Signs of decay and of new life in later Paganism.— The Hellenistic period cannot be severed by any sharp dividing line from the Græco-Roman ; but it belongs rather to the student of Roman religion and the Roman Empire to pursue the history of Hellenic polytheism through the first centuries of our era down to the establishment of Christianity. The religious phenomena of the period that has just been sketched present, on the one hand, the signs of decay, the decay of the old civic and political religion which fostered the growth of the Greek Polis, the intrusion from the East of demonology and magic, and on the other hand the working of new religious forces which prepare the way for Christianity. The cults of Apollo, Zeus and Athene were among the first to wither ; yet a living and personal religious sense was in all probability more diffused through the Greek world under the Epigoni and the Roman Empire than it had been in the earlier centuries. Contact with the Oriental spirit brought to many a stronger intensity of religious life ; religion is no longer preoccupied with the physical and political world, but its horizon lies beyond the grave and its force is ' other-worldliness.' Men flock to the mysteries, seeking communion with the divinity by sacrament, and sustaining their faith by mystic dogmas. The religious virtue most emphasised is purity, of which the influence is often anti-social ; this was no longer always understood in a pharisaic sense, but its spiritual significance was proclaimed to the people and penetrated the sphere of temple-ritual. An inscription from a temple in Rhodes of the time of Hadrian contains a list of rules concerning righteous entrance into the shrine, " the first and greatest rule is to be pure and unblemished in hand and heart and to be free from an evil conscience."[1] Something similar was inscribed on the temple of Asklepios at Epidauros.[2] The *objective* of the earlier Hellenic polytheism was the city, the tribe, the family ; that of the later was the individual soul ; the earlier religious morality looked rather to works and practice, the later rather to purity and personal intimacy with God, which gave the cue to the later ' gnosis ' and theosophy. The gradual divorce of religion from political life was a loss which was not repaired for many centuries ; but it was compensated by the rise of a humanitarian spirit which was to be infused into a new cosmopolitan religion.[3]

The above is only a panoramic sketch indicating the various elements of a singularly manifold religious system. It has been impossible to touch

[1] *C.I.G. Ins. Mar. Æg.*, 1, 789.
[2] Vide my *Evolution of Religion*, p. 138.
[3] Vide my *Hibbert Lectures*, Lect. VI, " Personal Religion in Greece."

on all the special points of interest, such as divination and the minutiæ of ritual and of the festivals ; for these the student must consult special treatises. The object of this monograph has been to present the main essential features in a chronologic survey and to assign to each its significance and relative importance. The history has been adumbrated of a religion that maintained itself for nearly two thousand years on the higher plane of polytheism ; a religion which, while lacking the sublimity and moral fervour of some of the Oriental creeds, made certain unique contributions to the evolution of society and the higher intellectual life of man.

By the side of the higher growths many of the products of lower and savage culture were maintained which were mainly obliterated by Christianity. It is necessary to note and appreciate these lower facts ; but there is a risk of overestimating their importance and vitality. Many of these are found in all higher religions, usually in a moribund state. It is its higher achievement that makes any particular religion of importance in the history of civilisation ; and we are now aware that Greek religion can claim this importance. Nor can the lower elements as a whole be shown to be the germs of the higher within the Hellenic period proper. We cannot show the evolution of the personal anthropomorphic deities of Greece from magic ritual or totemism or theriomorphism without transcending the chronologic limits of the period within which it is allowable to speak of a Hellenic people at all. The emergence of personal Gods, from whatever region or by whatever influence they emerged, is an event of very primitive history. At least we know that of the two populations whose blending made Hellenism, the indigenous Mediterranean and the Northern or Central European invader, the former possessed a personal theism of dateless antiquity ; while all the evidence points to the conviction that the Aryan tribes entered Greece with certain personal deities already evolved or acquired.

We find that anthropomorphism was the strongest bias of the Hellenic religious imagination ; and with this we associate his passion for idolatry and hero-worship. It is interesting for the student of Hellenic Christianity to note the influence of these tendencies on the later history of the Greek Church ; and generally it has been the result of much modern research to reveal the truth that the indebtedness of Christian dogma and ritual to the later Hellenic paganism was far greater than used to be supposed.

LITERATURE

OLDER works, such as *Welcker's Griechische Götter-lehre* (3 vols., 1857–1863), and *Preller's Griechische Mythologie* (2 vols., 4th ed., by C. Robert, 1887), are only useful now for their collection of facts.

Recent literature : O. Gruppe, *Griechische Culte und Mythen in ihren Beziehungen zu den orientalischen Religionen*, 1887 ; *Griechische Mythologie und Religions-geschichte*, 1906 ; L. R. Farnell, *Cults of the Greek States*, 5 vols. (1896–1910) ; Chantepie de la Saussaye, *Lehrbuch der Religiongeschichte* (Greek section, 1906) ; Jane Harrison, *Prolegomena to the Study of Greek Religion* (1903), *Themis, a Study of the Social Origins of Greek Religion* (1912) (both works dealing mainly with special questions and the more primitive aspects of the religion).

Treatises on special cults and special questions : Roscher, *Ausführliches Lexikon der griechischen und römischen Mythologie* (1884, in progress) ; Paulz-Wissowa, *Real Encyclopædie* (1894, in progress) ; and Daremberg et Saglio, *Dictionnaire des Antiquités* (1873–1917) ; Showerman, *The Great Mother of the Gods* (Wisconsin, 1901) ; Frazer, *Attis, Adonis, Osiris* (2nd ed., 1910) ; A. Dieterich, *Mutter Erde* (1905) ; Eitrem, *Hermes und die Toten* (Christiania, 1909) ; Immerwahr, *Kulte und Mythe Arkadiens* (1891) ; S. Wide, *Lakonische Kulte* (1893) ; Usener, *Götternamen* (1896) ; cf. paper on his theory in *Anthropological Essays presented to E. B. Tylor*, " The Place of the Sondergötter in Greek Poly-theism," by L. R. Farnell (1907) ; De Visser, *De Graecorum Diis non referentibus speciem humanam* (Leyden, 1900) ; E. Fehrle, *Die Kultische Keuscheit im Alterthum* (Giessen, 1910) ; cf. L. R. Farnell, *Evolution of Religion* (1905), Lect. iii, " The Ritual of Purification " ; Th. Wáchter, *Reinheitsvorschriften im grie-schischen Kult* (Giessen, 1910) ; C. Ausfeld, *De Grae-corum precationibus quaestiones*, in Fleckeisen's Supplement (1903) ; cf. L. R. Farnell, *op cit.*, Lect. iv, " The Evolution of Prayer " ; S. Reinach, various articles on Greek cults and myths in *Cultes, Mythes et Religions*, 3 vols. (1904–1908).

For Eschatology, Mysteries, Thiasoi, Hero-worship : A. Lobeck, *Aglaophamus*, 2 vols. (1829) ; E. Rohde, *Psyche* (2nd ed., 1898) ; A. Dieterich, *Nekyia* (1893) ; also *Eine Mithras-Liturgie* (1903) ; Jong, *Das Antike Mysterien-Wesen* (Leiden, 1909) ; Goblet d'Alviella, *Eleusinia* (Paris, 1903) ; Foucart, " Les Grands Mystères d'Eleusis " (1900), in the *Mémoires de l'Académie des Inscriptions et Belles-lettres*, xxxvii ; Pringsheim, *Archäologische Beiträge zur Geschichte des Eleusinischen Kults* (Munich, 1905) ; Foucart, *Associations religieuses chez les Grecs* (1873) ; L. Weniger, *Ueber das Collegium der Thyiaden* (1876) ; Article on " Héros," by Deneken, in Roscher's *Lexikon* ; Pfister, *Der Reliquien-kult im Alterthum* (1910).

Greek ritual and festivals : A. Mommsen, *Feste der Stadt Athen* (1898) ; P. Stengel, " Die griechischen Sacral-alterthümer," in Iwan von Müller's *Handbuch* (vol. v, 1898) ; *id. Opferbraüche der Griechen* (1910) ; Fritze, *Die Rauchopfer bei den Griechen* (1894) ; L. R. Farnell, " Sacramental Communion in Greek Religion," *Hibbert Journal* (1903) ; M. P. Nillson, *Griechische Feste* (1906), also *Studia de Dionysiis Atticis* (1900) ; Foucart, *Le culte de Dionysos en Attique* (1904) ; A. Thomsen, " Der Trug des Prometheus," in *Archiv für Religions-Wissenschaft* (1909) ; Rouse, *Greek Votive Offerings* (1902) ; Bouché-Leclerq, *Histoire de la divination* (4 vols. 1879–1881) ; Deubner, *De Incubatione* (1900) ; E. Samter, *Geburt Hochzeit und Tod* (1911).

Greek religious thought and speculation : L. Campbell, *Religion in Greek Literature* (1898) ; Caird, *Evolution of Theology in the Greek Philosophers* (2 vols., 1900–1902) ; J. Adam, *The Religious Teachers of Greece* (1908) ; Decharme, *La critique des traditions religieuses chez les Grecs des origines au temps de Plutarque* (1904).

Epigraphic material : *Corpus Inscriptionum Graecarum* (passim) ; special collections of inscriptions bearing on Greek religion : Dittenberger, *Sylloge* (vol. 2), " Res Sacrae " ; J. von Prott and L. Ziehen, *Leges Graecorum sacrae e titulis collectae* (1896–1906, in progress).

Religious monuments : Overbeck, *Griechische Kunst Mythologie* (1871–1887, unfinished) ; L. R. Farnell, *Cults ;* J. Harrison, op. cit. ; Baumeister, *Denkmäler des klassischen Alterthums* (1885–1888) ; Roscher, op. cit. ; Daremberg-Saglio, op. cit. ; C. Bötticher, *Über den Baumkultus der Hellenen und Römer* (1856).